INNERPOWERMENT

MY JOURNEY ON THE PATH
TO HEALING AND SELF-MASTERY

WENDY BENNING SWANSON

Innerpowerment
My Journey on the Path to Healing and Self-Mastery

Innerpowerment with Wendy Benning Swanson
Saint Paul, MN 55110
wendybenningswanson.com

ISBN: 979-8-218-71061-3

Book Design by Transcendent Publishing | TranscendentPublishing.com
Editing by Mary Rembert
Author Photography by Megan Engeseth Photography

Printed in the United States of America.

"The privilege of a lifetime is to become
who you truly are."
–Carl Jung

CONTENTS

DEDICATION

To my husband, for always supporting me in being who I am, even when you don't fully understand what I'm doing.

To my children, for constantly teaching and inspiring me and for bringing your light into my life.

To my mother-in-law, Kris, for your openness and willingness to try every new healing modality I offer.

To the Benning family for being a cherished part of my journey.

To my local Spiritual family for creating the unity we want to see in the world. I am so honored to be on this path with you.

To my US-based and International Spiritual Family, I am so grateful to be on this path with you, and I can't wait to see what we create!

LETTER TO THE READER

I was once in your shoes. I thought I was doing my best—striving in the world, climbing the "success" ladder, but I could not understand why I wasn't happy or fulfilled.

Despite my efforts, I was constantly tired, stressed, and found little joy in life. It took a tragedy to wake me up and help me realize that I am so much more than just this physical body. There's a bigger picture at play, one we're never taught to see.

For years, I searched for "happiness," believing it was something outside myself. But the real revelation came when I discovered that it wasn't happiness I was looking for, but JOY, and it was already within me. I was the one responsible for unlocking it. No one else could do that for me.

For so long, I felt out of control, believing I had to live for others' approval just to feel good. But the truth is, I was in control the entire time! I just needed to heal my relationship with myself.

The first step? Understanding who I am at my core. Once I began to truly know myself, I could finally start living from that place—and everything changed. You do not have to live in fear, anxiety, depression, or grief anymore. You can live an empowered life, fully embracing the wholeness of who you are, living with purpose and joy—every single day.

Join me on this journey to know yourself as the God or Goddess of Light that you are! My hope for you, through this book, is to take a deep look at the life you are living.

Are you in joy?

Do you feel a sense of purpose?

Do you wake up excited to see what life has in store?

Or are you yearning for something greater, knowing deep down that you are meant for more?

This book is for you. I intend to inspire you to embark on your own journey toward understanding who YOU truly are.

INTRODUCTION

I own a business called Innerpowerment with Wendy Ben-ning Swanson, and I have decided to author a book to share the transformative power of Empowerment and Self-Mastery, deeply rooted in ancient wisdom, sacred healing techniques, and powerful initiations that have been passed down through the ages. My goal is to demonstrate how these principles can enhance your life, bringing the joy and inner peace you may be searching for.

In this book, I will recount my life experiences, including the tragedy I experienced and how I transformed with the healing modalities I now offer. The healing, growth, and transformation I have undergone are so profound that they are difficult to encapsulate in a brief conversation. I have often found it challenging to fully convey the depth of my healing journey in just a few moments with a potential client.

I feel compelled to share my story because I have not found anything else that provides a clear path to joy and inner peace—qualities that humanity desperately seeks amid the pain and suffering in the world. I recognize that countless classes, modalities, books, teachings, and healings are available, making it difficult to discern what will truly work. Many approaches seemed effective briefly, but left me reverting to my previous state.

That changed when I encountered the healing modalities offered and taught by the Modern Mystery School. These modalities provided lasting change, and each healing or initiation I experienced built upon the last, leading me to feel whole and fully myself. I gained a clearer understanding of my place in this world.

This book will outline my journey and the changes I underwent. I understand that everyone's path is unique; some individuals may find that a single healing session is all they need, while others, like myself, continue to evolve and wish to share these healings with others as part of their service to humanity.

We are all unique beings, each bringing our special magic to the world. My work is rooted in ancient modalities tested over thousands of years, and significant efforts have been made to preserve their purity and light.

This book will inspire you to reevaluate and question your life. Are you living with joy? Do you have a sense of purpose? Do you wake up each day eagerly anticipating what life has in store for you? Are you actively seeking something more?

Some individuals find contentment in their routine, mundane existence, but many of you sense that a greater yet elusive purpose is waiting to be discovered. This book is for you!

My intention is that you embark on this journey with me and find inspiration to initiate your path toward the inner light and understanding of who you truly are.

THE DARKNESS WITHIN

On that fateful day in April 2009, I received a life-altering phone call while I was at work, where I shared an office with another salesperson.

Earlier that day, my co-worker overheard a phone conversation between my husband, Steve, and me. We were discussing a troubling issue, and although the conversation grew tense for a moment, we ended it with love and understanding.

I had no idea that just hours later, everything would change. That afternoon, I received a call from my brother-in-law, Mike, who delivered devastating news: Steve had passed away due to accidental carbon monoxide poisoning.

Describing the state of my consciousness upon hearing those words over the phone in a bustling office is challenging. My colleagues could see the distress on my face, but my thoughts were fixated on getting home.

I couldn't fathom that what I had been told was true; it felt impossible to believe. My brother-in-law's voice was filled with sorrow, but a glimmer of hope lingered in my mind, praying it wasn't real.

I hastily jumped into my car, and after mentioning his name, a couple of compassionate colleagues followed suit, noticing my distress. That drive home felt like an eternity, even though it usually took only half an hour. I wasn't fully present in my mind or body; I existed in a state of disbelief, questioning whether this nightmare was genuinely happening to me.

Then, a call from the daycare added another layer of complexity. They informed me that my brother-in-law had arrived, attempting to pick up my son, Chase. I assured them it was okay, but they were understandably upset due to Mike's distraught state, which, in turn, deeply affected Chase.

It all became overwhelming, and at that moment, my brain struggled to comprehend what awaited me at home. Time seemed to stand still; it felt like I had left Earth. Holding myself together was nearly impossible, as I was facing the worst nightmare imaginable.

Upon arriving home, they were in the process of taking my husband's body away. They asked if I wanted to see him, but I declined, mainly because I saw my mother after she had passed, and it wasn't her, so I knew that he wouldn't be there either, and I didn't want to experience that again.

Numerous questions followed, and then they left me alone on my front steps, a stark reminder of the profound loss I had just experienced. It's difficult to articulate my emotions at that moment: confusion, disbelief, and an overwhelming sense of "why." My mind raced with thoughts about what to do next.

Shortly after, my brother-in-law arrived with my one-year-old son, who had no comprehension of the tragedy that had unfolded. He greeted me with innocent joy, wanting nothing more than to play.

Soon, my colleagues and family began to arrive, and for an entire week, our house was filled with a constant stream of family and friends offering their support.

The funeral came and went, and eventually, everyone returned to their lives, leaving me to grapple with the stark reality of being on my own, with immense emptiness because all my dreams had been shattered in an instant. Two weeks previously, I was living a wonderful life with a husband and our one-year-old son, and now I was a single mother.

I chose to spend some time at a family friend's ranch in Wyoming, seeking solace and space to confront the overwhelming reality of my situation: I was utterly alone and solely responsible for a small child. While I knew I possessed a strong will to persevere and had faced adversity before, particularly with my mother's battle with colon cancer and her passing a year and a half prior, this was an entirely different challenge.

The grief from my mother's loss compounded the weight of my circumstances, surrounding me like an inescapable prison. For an extended period, it felt like there was no way out or respite.

Each morning, I awoke to a world that seemed to continue as if nothing had happened. News anchors wore cheerful smiles, people bustled about the city, and life appeared unchanged. Yet, something significant had occurred, something that had shattered my world.

While everyone else continued forward, I struggled to reconcile my existence without him. My entire reality had shifted, but it remained unchanged for everyone else. The people I interacted with seemed to move through life as if nothing had occurred, which only intensified my isolation.

Sleep eluded me at night, and each morning, I hoped against hope that it had all been a terrible dream. But the painful reality remained—it had happened.

Moreover, when I ventured into the world and encountered people who knew of my loss, many of them faltered in their attempts to be around me. They didn't know what to say, or their well-intentioned words often missed the mark. In their grief, they leaned on me for support, leaving me to suppress my grief to assist them.

Then, after I relocated from my home to an apartment, my cat's behavior took a strange turn. This feline companion had been a heartfelt gift from my husband and a constant source of solace during my period of grief.

Deep concern enveloped me as I sensed something was wrong with him. The night in question happened to be a Friday evening, and no one was able to help except my brother-in-law, who quickly came over to look after my son while I rushed my ailing cat to the emergency veterinary clinic.

The prognosis delivered by the veterinarian was grim; there was little I could do to ease my cat's suffering, for he was on the brink of passing away. They recommended that I make the difficult decision to euthanize him and put an end to his pain.

It was a moment that plunged me to my lowest point. Isolated, already submerged in profound grief, and devoid of any immediate support, I felt a profound sense of loneliness. There I sat beside my only remaining companion, bearing witness to the fading spark of his life.

Overwhelmed by sorrow, I retreated to my car and cried out in frustration, asking, "Why? Why must all of this happen to me?" It was as if I had been cast adrift in a world devoid of hope, shrouded in darkness.

Amid this abyss, my son emerged as a faint glimmer of hope, but burdening him with the responsibility of being my sole source of light felt unfair. It seemed like I had fallen into an even deeper chasm of despair.

Suddenly, a voice resonated within my mind, assuring me that everything would eventually be okay. It whispered that Indiana, my cat, was at peace, and I would emerge from this darkness. At that moment, I felt a tingling, luminous sensation in my toes, a warmth that slowly ascended through my body until it enveloped my head. When it subsided, I felt cleansed of the profound grief that had engulfed me just moments before.

I realized that I could muster the strength to drive home, take one step at a time toward a new day, and then another, and another. While the grief hadn't entirely dissipated, there was an illuminated path forward. It was an experience I could only describe as grace, something almost angelic. It marked the beginning of my journey toward rediscovering my inner strength.

THE CALL FOR TRANSFORMATION

As I worked to get a hold of this new life I was living, there was my son, a bright and happy one-year-old filled with boundless energy and a love for meeting new people. His infectious joy made it nearly impossible to remain submerged in my grief when he was near. He possessed a sense of humor strikingly similar to his father's, which fascinated and delighted me.

As he grew, he consistently found ways to make me laugh and giggle, a trait entirely his own. I often pondered what would have become of me without him, for he swiftly became my reason for rising each morning. I couldn't afford to hide under the covers all day, with him needing me to be present. I had to find a way to move forward, and it was because of him that I did.

As he continued to grow and began speaking around the ages of 2 to 3, he would mention seeing his dad from time to time. Initially, I brushed it off as childhood imagination, but upon reflection, I realized he had no grasp of ghosts or spirits. It became challenging to dismiss his claims as mere fabrication.

One weekend, after he returned from his grandparent's house, I inquired about his weekend. He casually mentioned, "It was good; I saw my Dad." This piqued my curiosity, so I asked where he had seen him. He replied, "He was standing next to Grandpa, and then he disappeared."

I attempted to ask more questions, but he fell silent, refusing to answer my queries. Up until this point, I had never believed in ghosts or life after death, viewing them more as a result of religious conditioning rather than a tangible reality.

Another peculiar development was the recurring appearance of feathers in unusual places, which friends and family attributed to signs from my late husband. These feathers would materialize in odd locations—perhaps a substantial feather on a pillow inside someone's home when they were thinking of him or appearing during the winter when bird activity was limited. Some even seemed to be placed in unusual positions.

Despite these occurrences, I remained skeptical. My scientific background led me to demand proof. How could Chase actually be seeing his late father? I initially regarded it as a child's fantasy about his dad and the feathers as mere wishful thinking, believing it scientifically implausible.

However, these unusual occurrences persisted. As my son grew older, he began claiming to see his uncle, my husband's identical twin, even when his uncle was over a thousand miles away. At one point, he mentioned seeing my mother, whom he had never met, asking where his uncle and the older lady had gone as we drove home from a family friend's house.

These experiences left me deeply contemplative about the nature of existence after death. Where do we go when we die? How do we get there? Why was my son apparently interacting with departed loved ones, and what were they trying to convey?

Could I, too, communicate with them? Were they attempting to reach out to me or send me messages?

I yearned to believe there was more to life than the physical realm, but how could I prove it? After all, none of us can truly know what happens after we die because we are still alive, right?

During that period, I began to experience inexplicable occurrences. One night, after an extended bout of sadness during which I had been crying for a long time, my home phone rang—an unusual event since I had never shared that number with anyone.

When I picked up the receiver, all I heard was static. However, strangely enough, that static served as a much-needed jolt to pull me out of the deep depression that had ensnared me. Could it have been my late husband trying to communicate from beyond?

Following that incident, I started noticing feathers appearing in unexpected places. They would manifest in unlikely locations, like beneath my table at a restaurant, in the middle of a ballroom, or in a hotel room—places where feathers are not typically found. This left me wondering if these were signs, perhaps messages from my late husband, reaching out to me from wherever he now resided.

I finally decided to seek a medium who could connect with my departed family members and provide insights into their intentions. I needed to determine whether this was a genuine phenomenon or merely a product of my imagination. Could the medium possess knowledge about them that would demonstrate their presence?

This marked a significant turning point for me—an active step I could take to gain some understanding of the inexplicable experiences I was encountering. It was a move toward dispelling uncertainty that had lingered for far too long.

I was brimming with excitement as I prepared to meet the medium. How would I know if she could genuinely communicate with my late husband and mother? How could I discern if it was real and what was happening when they spoke with her?

My mind was awash with questions, but there was an even greater sense of hope that I might finally receive a sign from my departed loved ones. The notion that they might not be truly gone was almost inconceivable, yet it offered a profound sense of solace.

The interaction took place over the phone, a detail that struck me as peculiar but ultimately acceptable. During our conversation, the medium shared numerous insights. She described my husband in intricate detail, delving into his personality, and conveyed his pride in how I had navigated the challenges life had thrown at me. It was precisely what I needed: a spark of reassurance, a new beginning.

This experience opened an entirely different realm for me, which had previously felt off-limits in some ways and shrouded in mystery. It was as though society had cautioned against venturing into this domain, deeming it socially unacceptable, or religious doctrines had discouraged it. But I couldn't help but wonder why. Why was it considered taboo? What was the potential harm? This marked the beginning of my journey to uncover and comprehend the Mysteries of Life.

CROSSING THE THRESHOLD

I found myself navigating unfamiliar terrain. Suddenly, my beliefs about the world underwent a profound shift. I yearned to comprehend the workings of mediums, to unravel the mystery behind their abilities and knowledge. What distinguishes a medium from a psychic? Armed with a scientific background and raised by a veterinarian father, I was ingrained with the ethos of understanding how things functioned rather than blindly accepting them.

My quest for answers led me to online research, but disappointingly, at this point, the digital realm yielded muddled information. The mystique surrounding these topics intrigued me. Why the secrecy? Why the hushed tones when discussing them? Frustration grew as I encountered a dearth of online explanations. Balancing a full-time job, the journey for answers progressed slowly.

When I entered the realm of spirituality in the early 2000s, I discovered a veiled landscape. Undeterred, I turned to books, stumbling upon Wayne Dyer's *The Power of Intention*. This book introduced me to the concept that unseen forces awaited my intentions, ready to guide me toward my desires. Embracing the idea of free will, I realized I needed clarity on my desires to harness these forces effectively.

After losing my husband, I contemplated happiness and used the power of intention to manifest a life partner. Crafting a list of qualities, I included playful challenges like romance and an Australian origin. Skeptical yet hopeful, I witnessed a serendipitous encounter with an Australian man in Las Vegas, marking the beginning of a storybook romance.

Despite the uncanny alignment with my intention list, cracks appeared in the fairy tale. I hadn't fully contemplated the subtler yet crucial aspects of what I wanted. It was a powerful testament to the potential of intention and manifestation, proving that I held the reins to shape my life.

Subsequently, I applied this newfound understanding and met my husband, who effortlessly met every criterion. This transformative journey is detailed in my book, *Finding Joy After Loss: My Journey Through Grief*, available on Amazon and other online platforms.

This experience illuminated my innate ability to manifest desires. Previously, I perceived life as random; now, I grasped that I could actively shape my reality. Despite my scientific inclination, explanations were elusive. The "Law of Attraction" was the closest match, emphasizing the role of thoughts in shaping reality.

As I reflect on this journey, I recognize it as a path of self-discovery—knowing myself, defining my desires, and realizing the power of creation. Initially daunting, the realization that I created my reality ushered in a new chapter. Uncertainty loomed: What did I want to create? Meeting a wonderful man was a positive outcome, but the deeper questions persisted.

In hindsight, this period marked the initiation of my quest to "Know thyself":

Who am I really?
What did I want my life to be?
What did I want to create?

These seemingly simple questions mirrored the essence of a wish. Inspired, I started my business, Verum Staffing (later changed to Verum Technical), to foster integrity and trust. My mission extended beyond personal success, aiming to inspire my son and prove skeptics wrong.

Life unfolded in the interim between my remarriage, the establishment of my staffing firm, the addition of another child to my family, and my father's battle with dementia that necessitated caretaking. The whirlwind of existence during that period left scant room for personal growth and development.

As time passed, an internal void persisted despite external appearances suggesting a prosperous businessperson with a thriving enterprise, a contented family, and a circle of friends. Joy and zest for life gradually waned, and I found myself unconsciously grappling with deep-seated grief. The eruptions of these unresolved emotions revealed an unfamiliar version of myself, leaving me puzzled about their origin.

While on the surface, I had seemingly achieved success with a flourishing business and a fulfilling personal life, an intangible something was amiss—a profound abyss. Starting a business had been a pursuit I believed would bridge this gap, a means to prove my capabilities. The goal was clear: initiate and build something from the ground up, a venture exuding integrity and garnering admiration, ultimately leading to a lucrative sale and a contented retirement. This envisioned accomplishment held the promise of filling the void that lingered within me.

As the weeks, months, and years unfolded, I dedicated myself to becoming the best business owner possible. I actively participated in workshops, delved into insightful books, and joined business circles to seek guidance from fellow entrepreneurs.

Despite my relentless efforts, achieving substantial growth for my business proved elusive. Each year, regardless of my endeavors to excel, I found myself in a similar position. While it was satisfactory, I yearned for more ambitious aspirations to expand and elevate.

In subsequent years, I experimented with different strategies. One year, I hired a sales manager; the next, a consultant to scrutinize my business and provide constructive feedback. However, their advice yielded limited results. Despite implementing various tactics to foster growth, the needle remained stubbornly stationary. That's when I began to question if the issue lay within me.

Embarking on a profound personal journey, I sought self-improvement to identify and overcome the barriers hindering my business. I delved into an array of books, absorbing wisdom on not taking things personally, adopting power poses for daily strength, and exploring the tools employed by successful individuals. Topics ranged from the habits of highly successful people to strategies for personal and professional development. I voraciously consumed every book available, striving to metamorphose into a better person and an effective leader for my business.

I absorbed valuable insights from various sources, incorporating them into my business practices. I also fostered a culture of continuous improvement by encouraging my employees to engage in a book club focused on the *10 Habits of Highly Effective People* and fostering weekly discussions.

While these initiatives generated progress, a transformative solution remained elusive. In the unpredictable business landscape, certain factors were beyond my control. Despite hiring skilled individuals, success often depended on their ability to generate business opportunities, a facet I couldn't entirely influence.

Motivating and training employees only went so far; the responsibility of execution rested with them. The cyclic process of hiring, training, and potential rehiring left me grappling with challenges. While I recognized my team's potential, they sometimes failed to see it in themselves.

I experimented with various management styles—strictness, understanding, feedback, options, freedom—yet none felt entirely effective. Even introducing daily meditation and Qigong to reduce stress and enhance focus didn't yield the desired impact.

Self-reflection led me to question if the issue lay with my management approach. My early mornings were dedicated to meditation, exercise, and preparation, signaling my commitment to self-improvement. I enrolled in sales manager classes, sought feedback from colleagues, attended seminars, and engaged in business circles, sharing frustrations and receiving advice on different approaches.

The realization dawned that my desire for success exceeded that of my employees. Moreover, my concern for their personal happiness and success seemed incongruent with the typical expectations of a business owner.

I grappled with the understanding that my role was not that of a healer to a workforce that might not share the same aspirations. While I wished for each employee to find joy and success, I discovered their commitment to personal growth varied.

It became clear that my pursuit of their well-being was not my responsibility but theirs. This realization was challenging, forcing me to confront whether I genuinely wanted to lead a successful staffing firm without compromising my core values and life purpose.

REALMS BEYOND

When I was young, I would visit my grandfather's house and head straight to his bedroom. In the bottom right-hand drawer of his dresser, I found a mysterious round crystal ball. I loved gazing into it and rolling it around in my hands. The crystal ball was weighty, its surface adorned with nicks and dents, evidence of its well-worn history.

After my grandfather passed away, I asked my mom if I could keep the crystal ball, and it has been in my possession ever since. At that time, I had no inkling that crystal balls were used for divination or to see things for people; I simply cherished having it nearby.

During my mom's battle with cancer, she whispered a secret to me—one that felt like a precious family heirloom. My great-grandmother, she revealed, used to conduct séances with a crystal ball. The entire family would gather, and even her cousin shared the same mystical gift. After funerals, they would come together to try to reach their deceased loved ones.

My mom waited until I was in my 30s to tell me this, which made me wonder if she had been embarrassed or if it was meant to remain a family secret. I was curious why she waited so long, but this hushed revelation made me feel like a guardian of hidden knowledge, entrusted with something sacred. At the time, it was hard for me to believe, so I tucked it away deep inside.

My knowledge of my great-grandmother is scant; the discovery of a newspaper obituary revealed only that she and her husband identified as spiritualists. Raised to dismiss such mystical notions because my mother never talked about this growing up, I considered crystal balls as mere objects, shaped into a spherical form, devoid of any mystical power.

Contemplating seeing visions within the crystal ball seemed illogical and unattainable. As my logical mind grappled with the idea, I needed scientific evidence. However, life had other plans. It wasn't until my husband's passing that my perspective began to shift.

After my husband's departure and my son's claim to have seen him, I challenged my insistence on tangible proof. This prompted me to acknowledge that belief doesn't always necessitate concrete evidence. My son's genuine encounter shattered my skepticism, teaching me that, sometimes, the authenticity of an experience transcends the need for validation.

As my understanding deepened and I embraced the idea that our existence extends beyond the physical body—a fact that can't be proven—I yearned for more insight into the post-life realm.

Pursuing this knowledge, I expressed my intention by connecting with a local psychic medium renowned for her retreats and personal coaching. Through our sessions, she imparted valuable teachings about spiritual intuition and the fundamentals of mediumship, guiding me on how to connect with deceased loved ones.

We did some work with the crystal ball; it is a place to focus while you use your intuition with your question, but this was not a strength for me. More importantly, we dedicated considerable time to working through the profound grief that enveloped me.

Being a medium, she facilitated connections with my late husband, offering glimpses into his realm, although the information was often vague. His recurring message was one of enduring love but with a gentle urging for me to move forward in my life. While he assured me of his well-being, he emphasized my continued existence and the life I still had to live.

Understanding this sentiment, I chose to focus on my personal growth. Subsequently, I sought guidance from another well-known psychic medium with a national presence. She facilitated connections with angels and imparted techniques to invite their presence into my life.

Through her guidance, I began comprehending that I was more than just a physical being; I encompassed a mind, body, and spirit. Crucially, she emphasized that I wasn't a victim of my circumstances but a creator of my reality. Any feelings of anger, resentment, or frustration were reflections of my internal state, even about my late husband.

Moreover, she enlightened me about the support system comprising angels, guides, and other benevolent beings available to assist me on my journey. She emphasized that while my late husband's love remained eternal, he had his own path to traverse.

This realization marked a turning point, as I started to grasp that my journey was not solely defined by his passing. His death prompted a reevaluation of my life, compelling me to shift my focus from yearning to understand his whereabouts to introspection about my path. The messages I received from him and other spiritual guides underscored the importance of self-reflection and hinted that our paths would intersect once again in due time.

I appreciated the guidance of both amazing women and the knowledge and wisdom they shared during our time together. It helped me open up to a new world of understanding who I was beyond what society or religion had explained to me in the past. I also began developing my intuition and connection to my guides. However, I still felt that there was more. They didn't resolve my desire to understand my purpose and who I was at a deeper level, so I continued to search for more answers.

Within the next year, I came across an advanced spiritual training school. I desired to gain knowledge through podcasts, audiobooks, and listening to TV shows while driving—a way to learn actively. Open Minds on the Gaia Channel stands out with its diverse array of guests discussing spiritual themes, health, astrology, archaeology, and more. Most of these individuals may not be widely known, but they play a significant role in awakening new perspectives, awareness, and understanding of our world through their work in small businesses worldwide.

One of the notable guests featured was Dr. Theresa Bullard, an international instructor affiliated with the Modern Mystery School International. Holding a PhD in physics, she passionately explores the intersection between science and spirituality.

In her episode, she delved into Kabbalah, a subject I vaguely knew about from Madonna's involvement years ago. However, I was curious to learn more.

Theresa shared a profound insight on the show that resonated with me: Kabbalah has the potential to reawaken our full divine potential. The concept was a bit elusive to me, but it lingered in my thoughts. None of the numerous conventions, retreats, and books I had encountered explicitly addressed the idea of divine potential. The term intrigued me, and Theresa's discussion made me consider the possibility that we all possess untapped potential waiting to be realized.

She emphasized that the journey begins with a Life Activation and mentioned the existence of individuals worldwide capable of facilitating it. Intrigued, I decided to explore further by searching for information online. I found a practitioner in my city and signed up on the spot.

I didn't know anything about this person or this activation, but something within me stirred. It wasn't mental; I couldn't put words to it at the time, but I know now it was a deep desire for knowledge, wisdom, and understanding of my divine potential and the truth of who I am.

ACTIVATING MY LIFE

When I set up my Life Activation appointment, I already had experience with two spiritual teachers and felt fluent in spiritual matters. However, I knew deep down that this would allow me to reach the next level in my spiritual development. There was an excitement about it that came from inside me, but I also felt like it came from outside of me. It was as if my spiritual support team was excited that I finally reached this point in my life.

The day of the Life Activation came, and everything within me was excited for something. I had no idea what. For some reason, I trusted what a woman I heard on a Gaia show said about an activation that was available to me in my city.

Looking back, I probably should have done more research on what it was, what it was going to do to me, what the long-term effects were, etc., but my discernment, my intuition, and my knowing told me that this wasn't your average run-of-the-mill type of healing session.

It was not going to be a session that does wonderful things for a day or two but then you go back to feeling how you felt. No, this session felt like it would activate something within me that would change me forever, but I was not sure what that was.

At this point, I had been doing a lot of spiritual work. I had spent over 10 years healing the grief of losing my husband; I wrote a book about my journey that inspired many people to begin their journey of grief. I felt that I had done my "time" and knew a lot about spirituality, angels, and life after death.

Even though I knew there was more, I felt like I had done a lot of work on myself and had obtained a certain level of enlightenment about "spirituality." I had already received a certain awareness and understanding about myself and spirit. But what this healing activated within me wasn't if A then B. It was if A, then B, C, D, and a new unique symbol I had never seen before.

The activation itself was interesting. The healer did several new things to me, including toning, working with my energy structure in various ways, and using a crystal on the end of a stick that looked like a wand.

After the session, I felt good, but I can't say I felt anything profound at that moment. I trusted that something happened, but I went on with my life much as before. It wasn't until a couple of weeks later, when I left the Minnesota State Fair, that I noticed something.

What I noticed was that I had fun at the State Fair. The Minnesota State Fair, often called the "Great Minnesota Get-Together," is an annual event that is one of the most popular destinations in the region. It's held the week before Labor Day weekend, and daily attendance has gotten as high as 270,000 people per day.

When I say that I had fun at the State Fair, I didn't realize I hadn't had fun before. Going was not always my top priority; I liked going, but there were so many people, and it was hot.

This time was different, though. There were a lot of people; the day we went was a record-breaking day, but I was not feeling their energy. I didn't even notice them. I only paid attention to my people, my family, and the friends that we were with. It was as if my energy wasn't spreading itself all over the place but was contained, and I had control of it. There was a sovereignty that I had not experienced before. There was joy and an aspect of inner peace that I was unaware existed. I could not believe it.

At first, I didn't link the Life Activation to this new insight into myself, but it was so new that I knew it was more than a coincidence. Something inside of me had shifted profoundly, making me aware of how empathic I was.

Being empathic can be a gift and a curse. Empaths can imagine how someone else feels and understand the emotions and experiences of others. Still, we often absorb these emotions and feel overwhelmed with heightened sensitivity in crowded or emotionally charged environments. We can find it hard to disconnect from others and often carry emotional residue.

I had been this way my whole life, unconsciously connecting to everyone around me, absorbing their emotions, and taking them in as my own. I realized through this experience how much I was taking on other people's "stuff" and thinking it was my own.

For the first time in my life, I was connected only to my energy and realized that my energy was lovely. I didn't need to take on the energy of everyone around me. I believe that I did that as a safety mechanism. I wanted to be aware of what everyone around me was feeling and know if I needed to protect myself from them. I truly felt liberated from these energies that always made me feel bad and were not my own.

This experience isn't necessarily what everyone experiences with a Life Activation; it's unique for everyone. But in general, it reconnects us to our divine blueprint, who we came here to be. It has the potential to bring us clarity and forward movement in life. It can lift the persistent sadness, loss of interest in life activities, worry, nervousness, or unease about things.

For me, I came here to not be weighed down by everyone else's energy and expectations of me. I came here to be my unique version of myself, standing in the understanding of who that is. This was the first step on my journey to knowing who I am or stepping into my "Innerpowerment."

Innerpowerment is the name of my business and a word I created by combining "inner power" and "empowerment." The suffix -ment signifies both the action or process of doing something and the result of that action. Therefore, Innerpowerment represents both the journey of developing your inner power and the state of fully embodying it.

Why is Empowerment and Self Mastery, or what I would call "Innerpowerment," important for Spiritual Progression? Empowerment involves gaining control over one's life and making informed choices, while self-mastery focuses on controlling and mastering one's inner world. Together, these concepts provide a strong foundation for personal development and are crucial in pursuing spiritual growth and enlightenment.

After my Life Activation and becoming aware of the shifts it brought, I was offered another activation called the Full Spirit

Activation. Since the Life Activation had already given me more awareness and freedom, I was eager to try the Full Spirit Activation.

At the time, I did not fully understand what it did. The activation itself was unlike anything I had experienced before. There was a toning of a Tibetan chant during the process, which felt strange to me. I was open to it, but my logical mind couldn't grasp the purpose or value.

The practitioner used a different wand, focusing on the top of my head rather than the back. I was also asked to keep my eyes open during the healing, but the energy was so powerful that I could barely stay awake. I knew something was happening, yet my mind could not understand how or why.

When I left the healing, I did not feel an immediate shift. The Full Spirit Activation is meant to increase your connection with your soul, so its effects vary depending on how connected or disconnected you are.

After my husband passed away, I became angry at life and disconnected from myself. I didn't understand why it happened, and without guidance or structure, I unconsciously distanced myself from who I was because I no longer knew that person.

Trauma, abuse, pain, and suffering can cause us to disconnect from our soul, leading us to live from our ego, personality, or subconscious. When this happens, we lose touch with our divinity and true self, conforming to societal expectations rather than living authentically.

The Full Spirit Activation helps reconnect you with your soul and physical body, allowing you to become more aware of your physicality, senses, and how you treat your body. It grounds you in your earthly experience, awakening clarity about who you are and your divine nature. It also reconnects you with your potential.

The impact of this activation was subtle for me. I didn't immediately see how it influenced my life because I had been so deeply disconnected from myself. However, looking back, I can see that it sparked a desire to improve my physical body and the food that I was eating. Not long after that, I started a liver detox and read more about which foods were healthy and which were not.

I started reflecting deeply on my business. I began questioning whether it was truly what I wanted to do. I had invested so much time and money into it that doing something else seemed impossible. Admitting that I wanted something different felt like a failure, but deep inside, I was beginning to realize my desire for daily joy.

I also wanted my employees to experience joy. The job is mentally and emotionally challenging as a recruiter, and I wanted to create an environment that would boost their confidence and motivation. This led me to start offering my employees meditation and Qigong (a moving meditation similar to tai chi). I strongly desired to serve them at a deeper level and support them in leading fulfilling lives.

During this period, I also noticed that my focus was shifting away from the grief of losing my husband. While it was still present, it no longer consumed me. This newfound space in my being allowed for something new to emerge. It felt like my emotional cup had emptied, creating room for a deeper understanding of myself.

I decided to write a book about my experience of losing my husband. For the first time, I felt ready to share my story with others. I hired a writing coach and spent six months writing about everything I had gone through, waking up at 4:30 a.m. every weekday to write before heading to work.

The process of writing my story was incredibly healing. Each morning, I would meditate on the moment I planned to write about, relive it, and then write it out. By the end of this process, I found that I could talk about my husband's death without becoming emotional, even with strangers.

I also realized that I no longer defined myself by his death, something I had unconsciously done for years. I began to move forward, focusing on who I was becoming and what I wanted to create rather than clinging to my past.

With this new sense of clarity, I started to explore the potential in my life and business. While my business was doing well, with profits and good clients, I saw the possibility for more growth. I joined a president's roundtable, hired a fractional sales manager and CFO, and took courses on sales management to help me take my business to the next level. We analyzed the business and found that while there were areas for improvement, especially within the sales team and processes, the primary need was to find more business. So, I invested in a full-time sales manager and committed to growing the business further.

EMPOWER THYSELF

My life was moving forward, and I was making real progress in my business. I had written a book and healed a significant part of my past, which brought a deep sense of accomplishment and relief.

Still, there was a lingering feeling that something was missing. That's when I decided to take the next offering from the Modern Mystery School, a class called Empower Thyself. It's a two-day class with an initiation where you receive 10 times more light in your life. At the time, I didn't fully understand what that meant, but it sounded promising.

I had already tried many different approaches to personal growth, and since undergoing the Life Activation and Full Spirit Activation, my life had improved. Although I couldn't fully explain how or why, I knew deep down that something had shifted. I simply felt better than I had before. I decided that it wouldn't hurt to take Empower Thyself. I was excited to learn more about angels, and the 10 times more light intrigued me. Beyond that, I had no idea what the class was about.

As the day of the class approached, I felt a lot of resistance, and I wasn't sure why. I didn't know much about the class, and it wasn't cheap, so I wondered why I hesitated.

I had never experienced this level of resistance to a class before, and oddly enough, it made me want to take it even more—almost as if the resistance was a sign that something significant was on the horizon. In my experience, resistance often indicates big shifts are coming, and those shifts are rarely simple or easy. But what kind of shifts could be causing this much resistance?

A part of me didn't want to go through more changes. I had just reached a good place—I had healed from a traumatic period, was heavily investing in my business, and things were going well.

Yet, I've always been someone who doesn't like to stay stagnant; I believe in continually moving forward. Having lost loved ones whose lives were cut short, I don't want to be on my deathbed with any regrets. So, despite the resistance, I chose to take the class, trusting my intuition that it would benefit me in the long run.

I sat through the class with an unearned sense of superiority, convinced I was well-versed in the subject. In reality, I was so oblivious to my lack of understanding that I dismissed the material entirely and felt underwhelmed at the time, thinking that none of it seemed particularly groundbreaking.

However, we were introduced to new rituals and unique tools. My teacher/guide explained that these practices would bring more light into my life and help protect my energy from negative influences. Curious to see if this was true, I decided to try them. I also enjoyed the initiation; I felt a lightness and a sense of joy when the class ended, so I went home with a light heart. (Side note: Empower Thyself was instrumental in my journey, though I didn't realize it then. I wasn't ready for much of what was taught, so don't believe for a minute that it isn't the most powerful class you can take that I now teach. Read on to discover the true power of Empower Thyself.)

I had been waking up at 5:00 a.m. every morning to meditate, so I simply added the rituals from the class, which took just ten minutes, and incorporated a new meditation I learned called the Sanctuary Meditation as my main practice.

Not long after, something interesting happened—my energy levels improved. I felt more alive, and when I took a step back, I realized that people around me, especially at work, weren't draining me like they used to.

As an empath, I could always sense my employees' emotions, often picking up on their fear of not performing well. Recruiting is a tough industry, with a lot of stress around finding the right candidates for clients, and I hadn't realized how much of their emotional energy I had been absorbing. It was as if I could finally separate myself from them. This realization helped me understand that their feelings were none of my business, and taking on their energy didn't help run my business effectively.

I also became aware of the constant negative energy I was experiencing. The rituals I practiced helped alleviate this, but they didn't completely address my negative thoughts about my life.

It was interesting to observe the distinction between external and internal energy. The rituals helped clear external energy from people or the environment around me, but I still generated a significant amount of negativity internally through my thoughts about myself and others.

I was becoming more conscious of this internal negativity, but didn't know how to change it. In the past, I had tried using affirmations—repeating positive statements to myself daily—but it felt fake. If I didn't truly believe those things about myself, would it even work?

Morning meditation and Qigong helped, but the effects didn't last throughout the day. Negative thoughts would inevitably creep back in. I read self-help books and listened to Abraham-Hicks videos, and while I noticed small shifts, I knew deep down that they weren't enough to shift my overall well-being in a truly positive direction. If I wanted to work on healing this internal negativity, I should take a class called Kabbalah, which I will discuss later in the book.

Let's revisit the Empower Thyself class because I was completely wrong about its impact on my life—something common among many who have taken this class because of how powerful it truly is. Often, we're not prepared for everything it offers us.

This class amplifies all of our life experiences and enhances the journey we've lived so far. The teachings provide keys that unlock information within us, knowledge we were unaware of until the class. With these keys, we can open doors we never knew existed and walk through them with newfound understanding.

These keys are sacred wisdom and knowledge passed down through an unbroken lineage over the last 3,000 years, perhaps even in the previous 8,000 years. The lineage is an important aspect of the authority that this class and the healings hold.

But they aren't something just anyone can pass on. The person entrusted with handing down these keys must follow the path of initiation, becoming worthy of receiving and sharing this sacred knowledge in the same manner it was handed to them.

My old mindset would have rejected this outright: "What makes this so special? Is this just another attempt to control me? Why isn't this information available to everyone?" I was self-righteous and suspicious, always looking for the conspiracy behind it. "Where's the catch? Who's trying to manipulate me?"

I now realize that my skepticism stemmed from being deceived, cheated, and mistreated so often in society that I had learned not to trust anything or anyone claiming to work for the greater good. My unconscious belief was that no one could genuinely offer me the keys to my freedom. However, over time, I have come to understand that the lineage itself is the key factor in the legitimacy and integrity of the teachings.

The Mystery School tradition has existed for thousands of years, with teachings that trace directly back over 3,000 years to King Salomon himself. The Mystery School uses the spelling "Salomon" instead of "Solomon" due to the Latin transliteration of the Hebrew name.

In Latin, "Salomon" is the standard spelling for the King, aligning with the Hebrew root "Shalom," meaning "peace," and is the spelling that has been passed down through the lineage, representing a commitment to preserving the historical context of the teachings.

Unlike knowledge gained from someone's supernatural experience, a book, or a message from an angel or being, these teachings were developed by King Salomon to support humanity and have been preserved through generations, passed down from teacher to student through the sacred process of initiation.

For the past 3,000 years, these teachings have been hidden within secret societies and hermetic orders, kept from the public until humanity was ready. In 1997, The Founder of the Modern Mystery School, Gudni Gudnason, a high-level initiate and key holder of the King Salomon lineage, brought these ancient teachings out of secrecy and into the world.

Since then, the school has been dedicated to awakening humanity from the slavery of ignorance and mediocrity, guiding individuals to embrace their divine selves and rediscover the joy of truly knowing who they are.

I want you to notice something important here. Initially, I didn't think the Empower Thyself class was "groundbreaking," but it truly was. For me—and this may not be the case for everyone—I was disconnected from myself and not fully ready for the shifts the class offered, and I downplayed its impact for a long time.

It wasn't until I audited the class that I realized how much I had missed the first time. When I went back through it, I would ask my teacher, "Did you teach this information last time?" She would laugh and say, "Yes, I taught it exactly the same way." It blew my mind that I could have overlooked such essential information!

I remember when I first took the class, I already thought I knew the material, so it's possible that I wasn't paying attention as closely as I should have. But it was more than that.

I had received the information and even changed my life because of what was taught, yet my conscious mind didn't seem to grasp the full scope of it. It felt like magick because, traditionally, I believed my mind needed to understand something for me to change. But this experience was different—it changed me, even though my mind wasn't ready to accept it. At the time, the information was beyond what I believed to be true or possible.

The Empower Thyself class also offers you 10 times more light in your life. Light means consciousness, wisdom, and divine energy seeking to radiate and illuminate your path and the path of others you come across.

The light is an empowerment that supports you in directing light energy toward your goals and desires in life. After the class, I wanted everyone to have this empowerment, so I decided to help my employees improve their mental, emotional, and physical state by offering daily meditation and Qigong. I became aware of the immense negative self-talk that I had and wasn't aware of before. Now that I knew it was happening, I was empowered to do something about it.

In addition, there is a profound shift in energy that aligns individuals with the **Will of Nature**, the **Will of the Universe**, and the **Will of God**. This alignment is incredibly powerful because, before the initiation, a person's energy naturally opposes these universal forces, often leading to confusion, struggle, and resistance.

When a person is initiated, their energy is no longer directed against these cosmic forces but instead flows with them. This shift is transformative because it harmonizes the individual's will with the natural order of existence. It is so powerful because, before initiation, people unknowingly work against the forces of nature and the universe, creating friction in their lives. The initiation redirects their energy into the natural flow of the universe, allowing life to unfold with less resistance, more synchronicity, and a greater sense of ease. They stop "pushing against the current" and start moving with it.

Aligning with the Will of the Universe and the Will of God connects people to their higher purpose. It's like plugging into a more significant power source that energizes their life's mission and clarifies their direction. Suddenly, life feels more meaningful, as if they are being guided by something greater than themselves.

Once the energy shifts, individuals are **empowered** to make choices that align with divine will. This doesn't take away their free will but instead strengthens their ability to act from a place of clarity, wisdom, and deep understanding of what truly serves their highest good and that of others.

The transformation of personal will helps a person refine it to align with the universal will. When someone's will is aligned with God or the universe, they become more attuned to their potential and can easily manifest their goals. Personal desires no longer feel isolated or disconnected from the greater whole—they serve the greater good.

The initiation process catalyzes spiritual growth by removing the blocks and oppositions that often hinder a person's progress. As the individual aligns with these higher wills, they experience accelerated transformation, healing, and expansion.

Opposition to harmony and peace often creates inner turmoil and conflict. When an individual's energy is realigned with the Will of God, Nature, and the Universe, they experience deep inner peace, harmony, and joy. Life feels more purposeful and fulfilling because they live according to universal truths.

By participating in the Empower Thyself class and receiving initiation, the individual steps into a flow of life that allows them to co-create with the divine forces that govern existence. They become a beacon of light, capable of influencing their reality from a place of greater empowerment, connection, and love. This alignment benefits and positively affects the world around them as they become a force for the greater good.

If there's one thing you take from this book, let it be the decision to choose the Empower Thyself class—for yourself, your family, and your future. This class will bring more light into your life and support you on whatever path you choose. It will also facilitate healing across seven generations back and seven generations forward, impacting your shared DNA.

In these challenging times, we need more people choosing light and rising above the chaos of humanity. We need people equipped with the tools to navigate and transcend the negative energy that permeates our world, enabling us to walk the path of light as we move forward.

HEALERS ACADEMY

My teacher/guide recommended a class called Healers Academy as the next step in my progression within the school's teachings and training. I was hesitant because I did not see myself as a "healer," so the idea of attending a "Healers Academy" felt out of place.

But I couldn't deny the profound changes I had experienced from receiving 10x more light, so I was curious to see what 100x more light could do for my growth, particularly in helping me expand my business. It took me about a year from the time I took Empower Thyself before I was ready to go to Healers Academy.

At Healers Academy, after completing the training, I received an initiation to receive 100x more light. To be honest, I went for the light with absolutely no intention of using the modality they were teaching, known as Life Activation, on anyone else. After all, I was a businesswoman focused on growing my staffing firm, and I didn't see how this fit into my life. However, I believed in growing my company with honor and integrity, and I felt that the light had supported me in doing that.

It was a significant commitment to take this class. The event was in Toronto, Canada, and lasted five days. This meant I had to pay for the course, travel expenses, and a hotel stay. However, based on my previous experiences, I knew it would be worth it.

The class was held in a hotel ballroom, and I was nervous because I didn't feel I fit in with the "woo-woo" crowd. Sure, I had already dipped my toes into the spiritual world and participated in my share of "woo-woo" activities, but at that point, I was wearing business suits every day and didn't consider myself part of that scene. I was apprehensive about blending in.

As we gathered in the ballroom, I noticed an array of people: someone with a tattoo on their forehead, another with dreadlocks, one dressed in high fashion, but most of the attendees were around my age and looked a lot like me—here for a purpose, though not quite sure what that was.

The woman leading the group, Kate Bartram Brown (later recognized as a "Divina and Ipsissimus" of the school—a leader, though more on that later), was magnetic. She was professional, polished, and seemed "normal," which, oddly enough, was a thought I had, though I wasn't sure what I had been expecting.

Kate radiated confidence and power, and her energy felt completely authentic—there was no pretense, facade, or masks. I could sense this immediately, as I am naturally empathic and usually pick up on the energy people try to conceal. It was the first time I had encountered someone with such clear energy.

During one part of the training, I approached her with a question. She took my hands, looked me in the eyes, and said, "Oh, that's such a good question. Come with me, and we'll figure it out." She treated me as if we'd known each other for years, even though she didn't know me at all.

Another woman on the panel was Ann Donnelly (also later named a Divina). Each morning, as I walked into the room, she greeted me with the warmest, most genuine hug, as though we had always been kindred spirits.

The way both women treated me felt so genuine, so true. It stirred something deep within me, like an awakening that whispered, *This is how it should be. This is how we should treat everyone we encounter. This is the feeling we should give to everyone we meet.*

I later realized that they were truly serving me, acknowledging that I am God, which aligns with the school's definition of service. They treated me as if I were a Goddess like them, as though I belonged, fitting into this community of humanity that had come together at that time.

Looking back years later, it took a long journey of healing and self-discovery to understand how to stand in my power and recognize the divine in others. I had to connect with myself as God, through healing, teachings, and especially the Universal Hermetic Ray Kabbalah class. Only then was I able to truly serve another in this profound way.

The five days of the class were beyond words. While we were there to learn the Life Activation healing modality, I gained so much more than I expected. I learned the true meaning of being in service to another human being—genuinely promoting, affirming, transforming, and acknowledging their divine nature, as Ipsissimus Divina Kate and Divina Ann had shown me.

This class wasn't just about learning how to perform a Life Activation, it was also about understanding the school's mission to create World Peace, or as they call it, Shamballah—a Tibetan term derived from Sanskrit texts that means peace. They taught us that we must first create peace within ourselves to bring about world peace. This idea stems from Hermetic principles, the school's foundation, particularly the Law of Correspondence, which states that our inner world reflects our outer world.

Through Life Activation, we reconnect people to their divine blueprint, helping them remember who they truly are. Awakening their DNA ignites the divine essence within, empowering them to step into their highest potential.

I spent a lot of time reflecting on this. It sounded incredible, but was that what happened to me? At the time, I wasn't so sure. I felt changed; I was definitely different than before the Life Activation, but was I stepping into my highest potential? That part was unclear.

Today, I can clearly see that it did guide me toward my highest potential—and I witness it doing the same for my clients. However, at the time of my Life Activation, I was deeply disconnected from who I truly was and uncertain of my purpose. I was more attuned to others' perceptions of me and what they wanted me to be. This made me hesitant to tell others it could have the same profound impact on them. I was too concerned with what others thought and didn't want to seem "different" or outside the norm. Not that this is outside the norm, but at the time, I felt people might pass judgment because it's so unique. Besides, I hadn't planned on performing Life Activations for others; I was there simply for the "100x the light" they said it offered.

During the program, they explained what it truly means to be a Healer. They shared that Healers hold space for others, empowering those they serve while bringing forth the holiness and joy they've received to their clients.

In doing so, Healers help move the world closer to world peace. Something ignited when I heard this, though I quickly suppressed it. The spark was the realization that I actually wanted to do this—I wanted to support people, guide them to their empowerment, hold space for them, and contribute to world peace, which I was unconsciously doing with my employees in my office.

Yet, at the time, I was deeply committed to my business and the path I had already chosen. Becoming a Healer didn't seem like a viable possibility for me. I couldn't see how it could fit into my future, so I pushed that spark out of my realm of possibilities, at least for now.

I also learned about the path of progression for humanity that King Salomon created—a path now open to anyone willing to walk it, not just those who receive a tap on the shoulder. I discovered that by serving others, we support our evolution, and this journey never truly ends. It's a spiral of knowledge, understanding, and wisdom that we continuously step into throughout life if we choose to. I also learned that much of humanity is stuck in this spiral, and Life Activation is a modality that can help move people toward progression and away from stagnation.

As the days passed, the importance of service and the power of Life Activation became increasingly clear. The energy of the space was so powerful, so filled with light and beauty, that it's difficult to describe to anyone who hasn't experienced it.

After the initiation, when I received 100x more light, I felt euphoric—almost like what I imagine someone taking a strong opioid would feel—a profound sense of well-being. But unlike drugs, this feeling lasted a long time, without any crash or low.

POST HEALER'S ACADEMY

It's truly impossible to take Healers Academy and not come back to life completely changed. For me, the changes weren't immediately conscious because I wasn't mentally ready, and I wasn't connected to who I truly was at the time to understand them fully. But I felt good. Life became easier; I wasn't getting as upset about things as I used to.

And I now had a tool to help others—to be of service. Even though my initial plan was not to use it but to simply absorb the 100x light, I couldn't help but want to try it out on someone, almost as an "experiment."

My first subject was my mother-in-law. I'm lucky she lives with us and is always open to my offerings. She happily accepted the Life Activation, curious about what I'd been learning in Toronto for five days. I know I didn't perform it perfectly, and I was so nervous that I made a few mistakes, but it felt so good to offer this to her. I felt deeply reverent and joyful, grateful to do something for her since she has always selflessly given to me and our family.

Next, I offered it to my husband, who wasn't exactly excited and didn't fully understand what I was doing in Toronto. However, he was willing to let me perform the Life Activation for him.

Afterward, I noticed that both of them had less resistance to life. They reacted less, and things didn't bother them as much. They didn't seek out the Life Activation, so I'm unsure if they noticed the changes because they weren't necessarily paying attention, but I noticed our household had more joy.

A couple of months later, I had lunch with a friend who was struggling with her relationship with her daughter and feeling depressed. Since she was open-minded, I mentioned the Life Activation and offered it to her.

To my surprise, she agreed! I couldn't believe she trusted me enough to do this. When I mentioned my surprise, she said, "I would totally trust you with this!"

This was my third time performing the Life Activation, and I was improving. Still, I was nervous because she was paying me! What if it didn't work? What if I did something wrong? After the session, she said she felt good, and we went our separate ways. I was happy to have another opportunity to offer this to someone I care about.

Not long after, I received an email from her titled, "You are Never Going to Believe This." She described how her daughter had decided to spend time with her and even hugged her. Her relationship with her daughter had shifted—because she had shifted.

I couldn't believe it. I mean, I could, but I couldn't believe I had done that. The healing I offered created a profound shift in her life. It helped me realize how powerful this healing is and how much it can change people's lives!

But this was just one person outside my family, so I wanted more evidence. Another friend, who had been talking about divorcing her husband for years, mentioned that even her friends had grown tired of hearing her talk about it, but she still had never taken action to initiate a separation.

I told her about the Life Activation and how it had changed me, and she said yes, she wanted to try it. Again, I was floored! I wasn't a healer yet—I was a businesswoman. We met in college while getting our master's degrees in leadership. But she trusted me, and she, too, was willing to pay me.

About three months later, she casually emailed me that she and her husband were taking a "pause" and had decided to live in separate places for a while. They weren't ready for divorce but wanted to see what some space would do. This was huge! I knew this step was what she needed to push herself out of her comfort zone.

Over time, she divorced him and stepped into the life she had dreamed of. It wasn't an easy path, but it was the catalyst she needed to step into her empowerment.

Would she tell you that the Life Activation started her on this path? Maybe not. Many people I've activated don't make the connection between the Life Activation and what happens afterward—but that's okay. I didn't either for a long time.

Finally, another friend invited me to her home, and during our conversation, she shared that she was going through depression. I mentioned the Life Activation, and a few days later, she said she was interested and came to my house.

After the session, she messaged me that as soon as she got into her car and drove away, her depression was gone—another powerful result.

Since then, I've had clients sell art they never thought they would or start campaigns that go all the way to the courthouse, making significant impacts. This healing activates our DNA and ignites our lives, which is why it's called a Life Activation. And now, I had proof that it worked. It creates profound changes in people's lives.

At this point, I was humbled and began offering Life Activations to anyone interested. But many people aren't. That's one of the challenging things about humanity—so many people are living mediocre lives, thinking that's as good as it gets.

I understand that because that's what I was doing before my husband passed away. It took his death to wake me up and push me to want more from life. I wish it didn't take loss for others to realize that there's more out there—more joy and inner peace. It's possible, and I am living proof of that!

It's not an easy path, and not everyone who receives a Life Activation has a positive experience right away. The light shines on our life, and sometimes we don't like what we see. Sometimes, we might face challenges in relationships or with family, or recognize that our habits and ways of living aren't serving us, but the light is there to offer clarity—to activate our life to something better and more aligned with the light and life purpose.

UNIVERSAL HERMETIC RAY KABBALAH

During Empower Thyself, my teacher/guide talked about a class called Universal Hermetic Ray Kabbalah. She said it was a blueprint for manifestation and how light flows from the Source of its energy into the physical, helping us to reconnect to spirit here in the physical. It is a 12-month journey up the Tree of Life, and ironically, it was the reason I received my Life Activation in the first place!

By this point, I had forgotten that Kabbalah was what Dr. Theresa Bullard was referring to when she spoke about living up to our full divine potential. The idea of unlocking that excited me because the rituals from Empower Thyself had already made a difference in my life, and I was eager to see what this course could do. They told me it was like undergoing 12 years of therapy in 12 months.

We began the journey in January with a two-day class, stepping into the lowest part of the tree of life called Malkuth. Over the next 12 months, I experienced an alchemical transformation, moving from the lowest aspects of myself to the highest. This journey forced me to confront how I lived my life and who I chose to be. It raised difficult questions: Was I taking responsibility for my actions? Who was I, really? Who did I want to become? How did I want to live? Was I happy? What past actions did I need to heal? How much of my negative ego was running my life?

The path, often called "Know Thyself," showed me how disconnected I was from my true self. I was living according to other people's beliefs and expectations—but who were these "other people"? It wasn't my family or friends, and it dawned on me that it was likely a societal narrative I had adopted that told me what I needed to be to feel successful or liked.

The truth was I didn't even know what I wanted. I thought I wanted to grow a successful business that could hire more employees, support them, and create a thriving workplace where people were excited to come to work every day. That's what I believed my life was about.

But as I climbed the Tree of Life, I realized that these desires were rooted in an attachment to being seen as successful. I was driven by the need to prove I was capable and competent in business.

However, the deeper I went, the more I saw that I wasn't my business—I was far more than that. I understood that I was an eternal being, and this life, including the business, was merely a stopover for learning and growth. I began to see that I was the creator of my world and could create anything I wanted.

That realization forced me to pause and ask myself, "If I could create anything, is this really what I would want?" It was a tough question because I had never considered that possibility. It took me months to even begin contemplating that perhaps the business I had built wasn't the ultimate expression of what I wanted.

It felt daunting, as if I didn't deserve to even dream of living out my true purpose or that it wasn't possible to be who I came here to be. Could I really be of service to humanity? Could my work bring joy and inner peace to others while still providing for myself and my family? It felt like a distant dream, but Kabbalah opened that door of possibility for me. The light touched that part of my soul and kept it alive, even when it felt too far out of reach.

By the time I reached the top of the Tree of Life—known as the Supernals— Binah, Chokmah, and Kether—I had come to a profound realization: I no longer wanted to own a staffing firm. Through this spiritual journey, I was able to shed the deep attachment I had to my business. I had always believed that if my business wasn't successful, then I wasn't successful. My identity was tied to it so tightly that my entire sense of self-worth hinged on its performance.

Before this realization, I lived every day in relation to my business. If we gained new clients or made successful placements, life was great because my business was thriving, and that meant I was thriving.

But if we lost a major client or an employee quit, it would send me into a downward spiral. I'd internalize it as a personal failure, thinking that everything was falling apart, that I was doomed to bankruptcy and ruin. These might sound extreme, but they were the unconscious fears driving me.

This attachment blinded me to other possibilities. I could never imagine doing anything else; it was success or nothing. Before Kabbalah, I had no idea this was the foundation from which I ran my business.

For many entrepreneurs, this is the natural order of things. It's easy to believe that this constant pressure and fear of failure drives success. But at what cost? What is the cost of living in fear of failure instead of allowing something to flourish out of genuine passion? How different would it feel to build something because your passion fuels it rather than running it despite your fears?

I also realized that I started the business after my husband passed away to prove myself to everyone who doubted me. Many people said I couldn't run a staffing firm, and I had been passed over at my old job because my boss didn't think I had what it took to lead a large team. I wanted to prove him wrong. In hindsight, that's not the best reason to start a business.

I built a profitable company and sold it for a profit, so I proved myself to some degree. But about five years in, I came to a sobering realization—the person I was trying to prove myself to didn't care about my success. The whole premise of needing to "prove" myself stemmed from a deep issue of worthiness.

When I recognized that it wasn't about him anymore, the need shifted to proving myself to me. But I wasn't doing a good job of that either because, deep down, running this business wasn't what I was meant to do.

By the time I reached this point on the Tree of Life, I had completely detached from the belief that my business defined me. I could see clearly that I was not my business, and my business was not me. I was Wendy Benning Swanson, and my business was something I had created—it didn't determine my identity. More importantly, I realized I had built it not out of passion or desire but to prove something to someone else.

I craved a life driven by passion, waking up every day excited to do something I truly loved. I also recognized my creative power—I had built a business from nothing, employing 50 people. That realization was empowering.

About a month after completing the Universal Hermetic Ray Kabbalah program, I received a call from a business broker with a potential buyer for my business. Although I had received similar calls before, this time I decided to return it. The buyer was specifically looking for staffing businesses of my size, so I signed the contract and started selling my business.

It wasn't an easy process. The first buyer didn't turn out to be a good fit—his goal was to "Uberize" staffing, simplifying hiring to the point where it could be done through an app. I quickly realized he didn't truly understand the complexities of staffing, and on the day we were set to sign the sale papers, the deal fell through.

This was a tough moment. My employees were already aware that I was selling the business, and I knew many of them would leave because they wanted to work for me, not for someone else.

However, I leaned on the "middle pillar"—a concept from Kabbalah that represents staying balanced and centered. Thanks to the Kabbalah program, I gained deeper self-awareness and knew that this setback would pass and another buyer would come along.

Without the foundation Kabbalah gave me, I might have been a mess, potentially reconsidering the entire sale because the first deal failed. But I stayed calm. Sure enough, my broker found another buyer within a couple of weeks, and we signed the papers two months later.

At the signing, the broker even commented on how impressed he was with how I had handled the situation. That comment confirmed the "fruits" of my work with Kabbalah, showing how it had truly shaped how I faced challenges.

After completing the Kabbalah ascension, I was recommended to receive an Etheric Reconstruction session called Celestial Code. This healing is designed for those who have worked through a lot and are ready to let go of attachments, marking the end of a larger journey.

The session helps restore the proper flow to the etheric field, reducing resistance and offering clarity by removing blockages. We often hold pain, confusion, suffering, and trauma in the etheric blueprint of our physical body, and this healing allows people to move beyond the pain and memories that keep them stuck.

With everything that had happened in my business during the Kabbalah ascension, the most surprising revelations came during the Celestial Code session. As I was receiving the healing, I began seeing, in my mind's eye, moments in my life when I felt abandoned.

I saw myself as an infant, crying when my parents didn't come right away (they were good parents, but this must have happened at some point). I saw my teenage years when friends abandoned me and several instances in college when boyfriends broke up with me.

Then, I witnessed the more significant abandonment issues in my life—when my mom, husband, and dad passed away. I saw all of these moments floating away as the healing progressed.

At first, I found it interesting, but I didn't think much of it. I simply thought, "Great! I've healed from abandonment." It wasn't until later, when I started interacting with people, that I noticed something profound had shifted. A deep, unconscious pain was missing. When I would talk to someone I didn't know, I realized I no longer felt fear. First, I was shocked to discover the extent of the fear I'd been carrying when meeting new people. Then, I recognized that the underlying fear had always been that the person might abandon me. This unconscious belief had been one of the most painful experiences in my life, and I had avoided new connections because of it.

Kabbalah healed this core wound by reconnecting me with my divine essence. Before this, I spent my entire life feeling unconsciously separated or abandoned from my true source. I didn't even realize it. The final ascension of the Tree of Life connects you directly with God, with your source, and that connection was so profound that it changed my life forever.

GALACTIC ACTIVATION

During my Kabbalah class, the teacher also offered a class called Galactic Activation. You might be wondering what this class is about—I certainly was. Here's the thing, and I mention this because it might be challenging for some to grasp, which I completely understand. We are galactic beings. We are more than just our physical bodies; we originate from the galactic, from the vastness of space.

When I say we are more than our physical bodies, I mean that Earth is just a stopover in our journey—it's not the entirety of who we are. If that's the case, we must have come from somewhere else, and that's what I'm referring to.

In Healers Academy, we were taught that humans possess 12 spiritual and 12 physical strands of DNA. When you receive a Life Activation, 22 of these 24 strands are activated, while two remain dormant. During King Salomon's time, they sought to understand why these last two strands couldn't be activated and concluded that humanity wasn't ready.

However, with the planet's heightened energy, we can now activate these final two strands. This activation manifests in the Adam Kadmon, or the God-like human in physical form.

In the two-day Galactic Activation class, you receive an activation that turns on the final two strands of DNA, connecting you to cosmic and galactic energies. The class was fascinating, revealing aspects of humanity I had never considered.

It shifted my perspective on life, helping me see everything through a more expansive, galactic lens. While we are born on Earth, it is merely a stopover on our journey, not the entirety of who we are. This class helped me realize that we are not confined to our physical existence here on Earth but are part of a greater cosmic reality. It also made me reflect on what that means for living here on Earth day to day.

This new perspective led me to reevaluate many aspects of my life, including the toxins in our environment and food, raising children with more awareness of who they truly are, and running a business rooted in the light.

One significant shift was in my approach to nutrition. After the class, I became more conscious of what I was consuming, especially protein. I began drinking protein shakes every morning, adding various vitamins and nutrients. The impact on my health and vitality was immediate and profound.

Before this, I wasn't a vegetarian, but I didn't consume much protein—probably around 20 grams a day, which isn't enough for our bodies to function properly, especially if you're working out regularly.

Without sufficient protein, the body breaks down lean muscle tissue for energy. Protein is essential for muscle repair and growth; if it's lacking, your body can't build muscle effectively. It's also a critical source of energy, and without enough protein, your body struggles to produce it, leading to muscle wasting and fatigue. Protein deficiency also weakens the immune system, making it harder to fight infections.

In addition, incorporating protein into your diet can boost metabolism by increasing the thermic effect of food—the energy required to digest, absorb, and process nutrients. This means your body burns more calories during digestion, which can support weight management. It's also vital for bone health as it contributes to bone density and strength, helps stabilize blood sugar levels, reduces the risk of insulin resistance and type 2 diabetes, supports mood stability and cognitive function, and contributes to the strength and appearance of skin, hair, and nails.

While the class didn't specifically cover this, a light bulb went off in my mind about how I was living my life. This shift continued as I went deeper into the path, and the Galactic Activation helped me awaken to a deeper understanding of my physical body.

It helped me transcend my negative ego, which used to discourage me from doing anything to support my physical health. I now take various mineral supplements and vitamins to support longevity and follow the biohacking movement to learn how to optimize my health and extend my lifespan.

I also learned more tidbits about how to run my business in the light. I knew some of the information, but I learned additional steps to strengthen what I had already started with meditation and Qigong.

They weren't easy steps because they weren't steps that most people in society were used to experiencing, so I felt like I had my work cut out for me at the time, although this was around when I realized that I wanted to sell my business.

RITUAL MASTER

"In every moment of time, we are given the choice between LIGHT and dark, positives and negatives, good and evil. A WARRIOR of LIGHT learns to be wise enough to distinguish the differences and recognize the choices; they choose LIGHT, even though it is often the harder of the two. Our ultimate weapon is love, our shield is peace, our fuel is passion, and our goal is JOY."

–Sovereign Ipsissimus Dave Lanyon,
Essential Principles For the Warrior of Light

After the Healers Academy class, I had the opportunity to take another step on my journey called the Path of the Warrior. Deep down, I knew I was ready to learn more about myself and continue my healing process. I've always known that I was a warrior. Life has thrown many hardships my way—the death of my mother from cancer, the death of my husband, and my father having a long battle with dementia.

While going through these hardships, someone once told me I was a "prairie woman." He wasn't referring to the fact that I was raised in Cheyenne, Wyoming, but to the women of the 1800s prairie who had to be tough as nails to survive. Bad things happened to them constantly, yet they pulled up their britches and pressed on.

That is what I had to do in my life; I had to press on. But that is where I come from. My great-grandmother on my father's side was raised on the prairie in Baggs, Wyoming, in the late 1800s. She even had an encounter with Butch Cassidy, who stole her father's horses but later returned them. There's an old newspaper article from an interview she gave in her 80s where she shared that Butch sent her a message of hello long after he was supposedly killed in a shootout in Bolivia.

My heritage is a lineage of tough women who faced hardships and persisted. I now realize that my inner warrior has been with me all along, the part of me I tapped into when life got tough. On days when all I wanted to do was curl up in bed, my warrior self pushed me forward. However, this connection was primarily unconscious. I wanted to understand who this warrior really was and how she possessed such strength. Who am I—Wendy the Warrior?

When I first heard about the path of the warrior, I instinctively knew it was a journey I had to embark on. But it wasn't as simple as signing up for a class. There were intentional obstacles in the way, designed to ensure that those who pursued this path weren't just looking for another experience—they were committing to becoming a warrior of the light.

The financial investment was also significant and served a purpose: Did I truly want this? Was I ready to commit? My answer to both was a resounding yes, even though I didn't fully understand why.

I felt an undeniable pull toward the path of Ritual Master, a powerful force I couldn't ignore, but I couldn't yet grasp its significance. I only knew I wanted to make a more profound impact on the world. I wanted to support humanity in becoming greater and finding more joy and purpose in life. But to do that, I realized I first needed to find those things within myself.

Before writing this, I searched Google for the definition of "warrior." According to Oxford Languages, a warrior is "(especially in former times) a brave or experienced soldier or fighter," or, humorously, "any of a number of standing poses in yoga in which the legs are held apart and the arms are stretched outward."

I had to laugh at the yoga reference because, coincidentally, I've always enjoyed those poses. But as I reflected on the more traditional definition, I considered what being a warrior meant to me before I started this journey.

My understanding was shaped by images of Spartans and the movie *300*—warriors who fought in physical battles. This path wasn't about preparing me for a literal war. I'm a middle-aged woman, and that idea seemed absurd. But I realized that I'd already fought many battles in life, ones that didn't take place on a physical battlefield, yet were battles all the same. And I knew there were more to come. I was exhausted from fighting and worn out from the toll it took on me.

But I wondered, *Is it possible to face life's battles and still live in the light? Could I find joy in the midst of hardship?* Deep down, I believed this was possible. It was something I had been searching for—the ability to face challenges without always living in pain and suffering, to rise above and live from a higher vibration, a place of light, and a place of strength and purpose.

Reflecting on my unconscious desire to be a warrior, I recall a business training I attended at the United States Military Academy at West Point through my executive roundtable peer group. At the time, I was focused on growing my staffing business, and this program provided practical tools for becoming a more effective and inspiring leader, drawing heavily on military leadership principles that could be applied in business.

One part of the training involved navigating a pared-down version of a boot camp obstacle course meant to teach us how to deal with chaos, face obstacles, and remain resilient. While I realized how out of shape I was, what stuck with me was how much fun I found it and how energetically powerful one of the female trainers was. From the moment I met her, I sensed something about her that deeply inspired me, even though I couldn't put my finger on it.

Obviously, she had a career in the military, but that wasn't particularly inspirational to me; the way she stood in front of the room and conducted herself captured my attention.

Over the years, I've often reflected on why she captivated me so much, and I finally realized it came down to a few key reasons. First, she spoke about her discipline—waking up every morning to work out and run. I could sense how her strong physique contributed to the way she stood tall and seemed ready to handle any trial that came her way.

More importantly, she knew exactly who she was. When you looked at her or shook her hand, there was an unmistakable energy of strength and confidence. There was no trace of fear or anxiety in her. I had never met anyone with so much composure and self-assurance.

At that moment, I knew I wanted to be like her. But it wasn't a confidence that sought power over others—it was the kind of self-assuredness that says, "I know who I am, and you're not going to mess with me." It was the confidence of a warrior. Of course she had that presence—she worked at West Point! It took me a while to figure it out, but what I saw in her reflected what I wanted to be: someone with that same strength and certainty.

I can see now that I am a warrior through and through, but at that point in my journey, I was clueless. I had no idea who I was and was following these breadcrumbs because everything else I had done up to this point had created a positive change in my life, so I was starting to trust that this could too.

As I mentioned, there was a process to apply for the first Ritual Master class, which included signing an Informed Consent Agreement. This document confirmed that we understood the responsibility we had chosen to accept.

I felt some fear, unsure of what I was getting into. I wondered, *What does this really mean?* Years later, I realized how serious this commitment was and that it should not be taken lightly.

My initial reaction was suspicion: "Are they trying to manipulate me?" I feared signing my life away to something or someone who would control me. But that was just my negative ego speaking. The truth is the agreement was about informed consent. I was being made aware of the seriousness of the journey ahead and the need to respect the sacred knowledge I would be taught.

Once I recognized this, I had no hesitation in signing it because I knew deep down that this path was meant for me. However, I also understand that it's not for everyone. I know many people who had completed Healers Academy but were not ready to step onto the warrior's path or make that level of commitment. They didn't have the same calling I did; perhaps they never will. That's okay—this part of the path is not for everyone. But for those of us who are called, we know. There is no doubt that you are ready to accept the requirements.

The Ritual Master classes are taught by Sovereign Ipsissimus Dave Lanyon, the leader of Modern Mystery School North America. He is an initiated Knight Templar, leading the world-wide Order of the Warriors of Light, a High Priest of Egyptian Magick, a master of Enochian Magick, and a specialist in Viking, Celtic, and Egyptian Shamanism—among many other roles.

But these titles alone don't fully capture who he is. He is the first man I've met who balances respect, kindness, and the ability to push you when needed. He embodies masculine and feminine traits in a way that shows me he genuinely has my best interest at heart, even when it's not what I want to hear.

I've always seen him treat people with dignity and respect, and it's clear that he truly wants his students to succeed. He supports you in whatever way he can within his power.

After taking several classes with him, I realized he is the first teacher I've had who is exactly who he says he is—no masks, no insecurities. He's open to being questioned and even to being wrong, though he's usually right! He never inflates his ego to elevate his status.

Instead, he comes across as humble, funny, and deeply in tune with the class's needs. This makes learning from him enjoyable because he offers what we need, even when we don't realize it.

I can say without hesitation that he is the best teacher I've had. I highly recommend taking a class with him for anyone considering this path, if only to learn from such a wise and authentic man.

The Ritual Master classes offer profound sacred teachings that bring deeper knowledge and awareness to our everyday lives. Through these teachings, you gain an understanding of light and dark, good and evil, and the ability to discern between them.

One of the central lessons is the importance of discernment in shaping our lives. You also learn about commitment and self-mastery, which are critical for a warrior's journey.

Additionally, the classes shed light on the pollution of the mind, the lifelong programming and conditioning we've undergone, and the ignorance that prevents most people from truly knowing who they are.

Beyond these topics, each class is unique and multidimensional, tailored specifically to the students present. While this gives an idea of the subjects covered, there is much more to discover within each initiatory process.

It is a path that truly challenges you to know who you are. Before I chose this path, I would have confidently said that I knew how to choose good over evil, light over dark—that I was a good person who always tried to treat others with kindness. But as I reflect, I realize there were moments when I didn't speak up when I should have—moments where someone needed a voice, and I stayed silent.

These situations weren't always obvious or dramatic. Sometimes, they were subtle, like when people gossiped about someone at work. I knew it was wrong, but I kept quiet, allowing the toxic behavior to continue unchecked. I didn't stand up for what was right and have contemplated this deeply. It made me question my ability to protect myself and not be taken advantage of by my silence.

One moment that stood out was at the airport in Phoenix, Arizona. I was renting a car, and when I got to the front of the line, they had my reservation but told me the cost was double what I had agreed to.

I knew at that moment something was wrong, but I didn't say anything. I didn't ask questions, protest the extra fees, or challenge the situation in any way. Instead, I handed over my credit card without a word. I felt the need to speak up, but I stayed silent.

I have had this deep desire to speak up but have felt this deep sense of being silenced. I was told by an International Modern Mystery School teacher once that I was very strong and powerful, but something happened to me. Maybe someone told me I wasn't enough or too much, or they took my power, so I didn't stand in it. It made me stand in the back of the room, wear black to be invisible, or not speak up when I had something to say.

She said that the world needed powerful, strong people, so I needed to heal that aspect of myself. For a very long time, I felt powerless about this, although I had a strong desire to change it.

What held me back at the car rental? Was it the fear of making a scene in front of people? Maybe I overlooked something on my reservation? All those excuses were false, and I knew it. I had been walked all over, and for what? So someone could make a sale. I left feeling ashamed and angry, disappointed that I hadn't stood up for myself.

I was in my 30s at the time, a successful businessperson who negotiated deals with presidents of companies and was praised for my strong negotiation skills. So why, in that moment, couldn't I advocate for myself? Why was this happening to me?

This wasn't the only time, but it was a moment that stuck with me because I knew what was happening and let it happen. I carried this with me for years, questioning why I allowed myself to be treated this way. Why did I feel so weak? Why was my will to fight for what was right so feeble compared to others?

I couldn't answer that question for a long time. I wanted to be strong, speak up, and do the right thing. What was holding me back?

Why was I letting myself down when it mattered most? Because I didn't know who I was! Deep down, I believed I was what I appeared to be at that moment—weak. I had never confronted it. I had never gone deep into the shadows and the darkness to uncover what was there and bring light to it.

Through the path laid out by the Modern Mystery School, I would ask if that situation reappeared. There wouldn't be an internal struggle, wondering if I should speak up or push myself to do it—I would just do it.

Since I have taken the Ritual Master Training, I have become a Ritual Master and a Warrior of Light! As my Ritual Master teacher, Sovereign Ipsissimus Dave Lanyon, writes in his book *Essential Principles of the Warrior of Light*, "Those that go beyond simply looking into the LIGHT and choose to confront the darkness, expanding Light into that darkness (let there be LIGHT!) we call the Warriors of Light."

I had to expand light into my darkness. I had to confront the aspects of my life that made me feel powerless in front of another person. I had to understand that there is Light and Darkness, Good and Evil.

The New Age path I was on before the school had told me it was only light; darkness didn't exist or was somehow my fault. But that isn't necessarily true. If you don't know something exists, you can't address it. This is why the New Age path doesn't help people progress—it's missing a critical aspect of life.

I also learned the importance of discernment on this path. Without it, you're essentially a sheep—letting others make decisions for you. I had to stop following the crowd and allowing their choices to dictate mine, like only doing something if someone else was doing it or trying to fit in.

I realized that what works well for someone else doesn't necessarily apply to me, especially if the results weren't there. By "results," I mean the positive outcomes of my decisions.

A classic example for me was having a glass of wine every night with dinner. It never had any positive results—just stomach pain, headaches, and tiredness. My discernment showed me that this habit wasn't my best decision, so I let it go.

Being a Ritual Master meant I had to shift my way of being in many ways. One of the most significant changes was realizing how essential physical health and strength were to my mission as a warrior.

After my first Ritual Master class, I enrolled in a Warriors of Light training. I had no idea what to expect, and I was shocked to find that it involved hundreds of push-ups, sit-ups, squats, mountain climbers, and extended running sessions. It became painfully clear how out of shape I was, and the experience turned out to be incredibly tough and miserable.

When I returned home, I resolved to get stronger. At the time, I was in my early 40s and hadn't done much physical exercise since I was a dancer in high school. The only physical activity I had done somewhat consistently was yoga, which I had prac-ticed on and off for about 10 years. While yoga made me feel better when I stuck with it, I never saw myself as someone who would go to the gym and work out—I wouldn't even know where to start! To be honest, I often found excuses to avoid exercise altogether.

Once, in a business peer group, someone told me I was "skinny fat." The speaker explained that the term describes someone who appears thin or has a low body weight but carries a higher percentage of body fat with lower muscle mass. Despite look-ing slim in clothing, people with this body composition tend to have little muscle tone and may carry fat around areas like the belly or hips.

The term highlights that physical health and fitness aren't just about being thin but also about body composition, muscle mass, and overall strength. This can be misleading because people who are "skinny fat" might still be at risk for health issues, such as high cholesterol or insulin resistance, due to poor muscle-to-fat ratios.

Even with this information, I didn't feel pressure to lose weight or get healthier, as I had always been fairly thin my entire life. Looking back, I also remember being tired a lot, taking naps every day, and not having much stamina and endurance when lifting objects or walking long distances.

I also struggled when traveling when I needed to carry suitcases and other bags. It was a noticeable strain, which I thought was because I was getting older. I never thought there was a solution to it.

In January of the following year, I decided to try strength training. I joined a facility focused on evidence-based, peer-reviewed scientific research to utilize safe and efficient strength training techniques. The program involved just 30 minutes of high-intensity training once a week. Although they recommended two days, they explained that training once a week would still provide 80% of the benefit, so I started with that, unsure of what to expect. My initial goal was simple: to be able to do 100 push-ups.

The first few sessions were tough. My body was so out of shape that I was sore for days and had to take naps after the workouts because my body was not happy.

That was three years ago. After a few months, I wasn't as sore or fatigued, and I started noticing more energy in my daily life. After about six months, I no longer needed to nap after workouts. I couldn't believe that just 30 minutes of strength training once a week could make such a difference.

After a year of strength training, I added one Pilates class a week and started a Mixed Martial Arts class. That year, during Warriors of Light training, I felt stronger and could do all the exercises much better, including running. It's amazing how much easier running becomes when your legs are stronger!

The next year, I increased my Pilates classes to three to four times a week and challenged myself by running an 8K that Ipsissima Divina Franca Lanyon headed up with my colleagues at the Modern Mystery School in Canada.

Every day I trained, I pictured running up the mountain during Warriors of Light training, which motivated me to keep improving. Even though I suffered a hairline fracture in my foot and my ankles swelled and ached after every run, I pushed through and completed the race—a huge accomplishment for me.

As I approach 50, I've never felt better. Along with regular exercise, I've started taking vitamins and mineral supplements to support my physical body and eating more healthily by reducing sugar and increasing protein.

I also use Lumen, a device that tracks your metabolism by measuring the CO_2 concentration in your breath. It helps me understand how my metabolism functions and shows how it responds to different foods, offering real-time health data.

Additionally, I purchased an Oura ring, which tracks heart rate, temperature, and over 20 other biometrics throughout the day and night. It provides valuable insights into my sleep, heart health, and stress levels, helping me understand my overall well-being. These tools have shown me how my body is getting stronger and healthier as I continue working out.

It's interesting how sometimes it takes something deeper, like becoming a Ritual Master, to spark a real change in how we approach our physical health. I didn't truly value my body before, despite watching my parents face cancer and dementia. Even those experiences didn't drive me to prioritize it. The teachings and training showed me the importance of taking control of my health.

My body is my vessel for life, and if I want to be a true Warrior of Light, my physical health has to support that mission. If I'm exhausted, drained, or unhealthy, I can't serve or be fully present as a lightworker. That realization shifted everything for me. It became clear that this wasn't just something that would happen on its own—it was a process, an evolution, and ultimately, a choice I had to make.

One of the biggest changes was giving up alcohol and caffeine. It's shocking how much just one or two glasses of wine a day weighed me down, leaving me feeling awful all the time. I didn't realize how much coffee was constantly hurting my stomach until I stopped.

Now, I see how ingrained alcohol and caffeine are in society, and it's no surprise to me that people's physical health is declining. Personally, it felt like being freed from chains when I quit. It was like the clouds lifted, and I could finally see how much these habits affected my body.

So, I asked myself why and how these Ritual Master classes and initiations created all these changes in me. As someone who likes to understand how and why things happen, I was disappointed because I can't tell you exactly why or how. I took a class. I received an initiation. We learned some new rituals that I did every day, and the rest was magick (magick with a "k," which signifies a more serious, intentional, and spiritually focused practice compared to the more entertainment-oriented or fictional concept of magic with a "c").

The school defines Magick as changing nothing into something and something into something else. I changed into something else. Something more than I was before. More alive. More aware. I gained more understanding of who I was and my place in the universe. Was that just the Ritual Master class or the combination of Life Activation, Healers Academy, Kabbalah, and Ritual Master all working with and through me? Who is to say? But the point is that I have upgraded my life immensely.

AWAKENING THE GUIDE

After I sold my business, I was exhausted. It felt like a massive weight was lifted off my shoulders as I let go of the responsibilities that came with managing 50 employees.

For the first time in a long while, I had the space to just be, but it wasn't easy at first. For months, I still woke up early and struggled with the need to stay busy, as though productivity was tied to my very sense of being alive.

Fortunately, I was able to take a year off to reflect and figure out what I truly wanted next. At that point, I wasn't sure if I was ready to step fully into the world as a Healer. I understood the gravity of such a role and needed time to decide if it was really for me.

The next step in my progression within the Modern Mystery School was to be initiated as a Guide in the lineage. Being a Guide is a significant responsibility. It means holding the authority and power to initiate Adepts through the Empower Thyself program. It also means committing to serving humanity for the rest of your life.

I knew from the classes I'd already taken that this wasn't an easy path—it would be the most rewarding thing I could ever do, but it would also require courage and bravery to stand in the light and live life at the highest standard.

When I started taking classes with the school, I did it for the light. I felt the goodness and the shifts within myself after receiving the healings and teachings. These experiences were different from anything else I'd encountered—they lasted, continuing to affect me long after the sessions ended.

I began to ask myself if I could return to who I was before. The answer was clear: I couldn't. I had more joy and understanding of who I was and detached from false beliefs that once limited me. I felt empowered like never before.

As I began offering healings to friends and family, I saw the results firsthand. I knew this worked—I experienced its benefits myself and witnessed it in others.

Reflecting on my journey, I realized there was nothing else I'd rather do than help people bring more light into their lives. And I wasn't about to do this halfway; I'm either all in or not at all. So I had to ask myself seriously: Is this what I want for the rest of my life?

To gain more clarity, I decided to go on a pilgrimage to Avalon in Glastonbury with a group of women. We walked the path of the feminine, reconnecting with the ancient lineage of scent priestesses and reigniting the feminine power that had been dormant in me for so long.

It was an incredible retreat, especially the connection I felt with Avalon's red and white springs, helping me tap into the feminine aspects of myself that I had missed for most of my life.

But even in the beauty of that experience, something was missing. I didn't feel the lineage of King Salomon, the deep thread of wisdom, knowledge, and truth that has been passed down through the ages.

That's when I knew, without question, that I wanted to become a Guide. I wanted to fully commit to helping reignite the flame in others through initiation, healing, and teaching those who seek more light and a deeper understanding of their true selves.

I had seen firsthand the transformative power of this path, and I wanted to dedicate myself to sharing it with the world.

The Guide initiation is a powerful and sacred process. The teachings were transformational, and when I completed them, I deeply understood why I was drawn to this work. Now, I have the authority to initiate Adepts through the Empower Thyself class.

As you close this book, I hope you feel a deeper understanding of the transformative path I've shared with you. This journey isn't about following someone else's blueprint but discovering your own. Each of us is a unique expression of the divine, and the light shines differently for everyone, illuminating the next steps on our individual path.

My work as a healer, guide, and teacher is not about fixing or changing you but empowering you to unlock the wisdom and strength that already exists within. Through the tools, teachings, and healings I offer, I aim to help you reconnect with your true self, awaken your potential, and align with your divine purpose.

For those who feel ready, the path ahead is filled with opportunities to expand, heal, and grow. Whether you explore healing modalities, participate in classes like Empower Thyself, or embark on advanced spiritual work, every step you take is an act of self-discovery and empowerment.

The beauty of this path is that it meets you exactly where you are. Whether you're seeking to release old patterns, deepen your spiritual awareness, or find clarity in your life's direction, the journey begins with a single decision—to take the first step with a Life Activation.

I invite you to reach out if you feel called to continue your spiritual journey with me. Whether through a healing session, a class, or a conversation, I'm here to support you. Together, we can explore the tools and teachings that will empower you to create the life you desire—one aligned with your highest truth and deepest joy.

If you aren't local to me in the Minnesota area, there is a website that will help you find a Life Activation Practitioner close to you. That website can be found at the end of this book in the "Resources for Your Journey" section.

Remember, the light is always within you, waiting to be uncovered. Your journey is yours to walk, and I'm honored to walk alongside you, even if just for a part of it.

The question now is: Are you ready to take the next step?

AWAKENING THE NEED AND OVERCOMING RESISTANCE TO HEALING

Starting a healing journey can be one of the most transformative decisions a person makes. However, one of the most profound truths about healing is that many people don't realize they need it. Life's **challenges**, **stressors**, and **patterns** often feel so normal that we become desensitized to their impact on our mental, emotional, and spiritual well-being. People may think, "This is just how life is," or "I'm fine—nothing is really wrong," but deep down, they might feel unfulfilled, stuck, or disconnected from themselves. Recognizing the need for healing is often the first step toward transformation.

Signs You May Benefit from a Healing Path

If you have ever felt something is missing or wondered why life feels harder than it should, it could be a sign that healing is needed. Here are some common indicators:

Feeling Stuck in Life: You might feel like you are running in circles, repeating the same patterns in relationships, career, or personal growth without progress.

Low Energy or Fatigue: Chronic exhaustion, despite rest or self-care, can signal unresolved emotional or energetic blockages

Emotional Overwhelm: Struggling with feelings of anxiety, sadness, anger, or fear that seem disproportionate to the situations you face

Difficulty Moving On: Feeling unable to let go of past traumas, heartbreaks, or negative experiences, even when you want to move forward

Lack of Joy or Purpose: Life feels monotonous or meaningless, and moments of joy or fulfillment are rare.

Recurring Physical Ailments: Persistent aches, pains, or health challenges that don't seem to have a clear medical cause

Disconnection from Self or Others: A sense of being detached or isolated, even in the company of loved ones or within your body

Inner Criticism or Self-Doubt: Constant negative self-talk, low self-worth, or fear of failure holding you back

Resentment or Blame: Difficulty forgiving yourself or others, leading to bitterness or an inability to move forward

Curiosity About Something More: A subtle but persistent sense that there is more to life—more depth, meaning, and connection waiting to be discovered

As you've read in this book, I faced many challenges that left me feeling stuck in life. Emotional overwhelm consumed me, and I struggled to move forward after the passing of my husband.

For years, I felt a lack of joy and purpose while my inner critic and self-doubt seemed to weave into every part of my story. Yet, even amidst these struggles, there was always a quiet curiosity—a sense that there had to be something more waiting for me.

These signs weren't unique to my journey—they are universal experiences many people face, often without fully recognizing their significance. By sharing how I navigated these challenges and found my way toward healing, growth, and empowerment, I hope to inspire you to reflect on your path.

If you see yourself in one or more of these signs, let them serve as a gentle invitation to begin exploring your healing journey. Transformation starts with a single step, and the journey ahead holds profound potential for joy, freedom, and self-discovery.

How a Path to Know Thyself Can Help

Healing is not just about fixing what is "broken"—it's about uncovering your true self and rediscovering the innate wholeness within you.

This path offers:

Emotional Relief: Release suppressed feelings and lighten the emotional load you've been carrying.

Energetic Alignment: Clear blocks in your energy field, allowing you to feel more vibrant, balanced, and alive.

Spiritual Connection: Deepen your understanding of your purpose and feel connected to something greater.

Clarity and Focus: Heal mental clutter and confusion, making way for clearer decision-making and inner peace.

Empowerment: Learn tools and practices that help you take charge of your growth and transformation.

Awakening the need for healing often begins with a feeling—a subtle nudge that something could be different, better, or more fulfilling. If you have resonated with any of the signs above, consider it an invitation to explore what healing can offer you.

You don't have to take giant leaps—small steps, like starting a meditation practice, journaling, or seeking a healer, can lead to profound change.

Healing is not about reaching perfection; it's about becoming more of who you truly are. When you step onto a path of healing, you open the door to joy, peace, and the freedom to live the life you were meant to live.

TESTIMONIALS

Illuminating the Path: Kristin's Life Activation Journey

I walked into my Life Activation session with curiosity and an open mind but no specific expectations. I wasn't looking for it to solve a particular problem or fix something in my life; there wasn't a pressing issue I needed it to address.

Instead, I approached it as an opportunity to see what might unfold. During the session, I stayed present, fully participating, even though my only job was to be there. Afterward, I didn't feel any immediate changes—no surge of energy, no dizziness, no emotional breakthroughs. I just went about the rest of my day, wondering what, if anything, might come of it.

What I didn't realize was that something profound had already begun shifting inside me.

Since 2019, my family has been grappling with the devastating loss of my cousin, who was murdered. Around the time of my Life Activation, we learned that one of the perpetrators would receive only probation—a sentencing decision that left me feeling powerless and deeply upset. I felt trapped in inertia, believing that nothing I could do would change the outcome.

But shortly after the Life Activation, something unexpected happened. I started reaching out to others who had faced similar tragedies. I built connections, launched an online petition, and created a website to draw attention to our cause.

None of this was typical for me—I've never been the type to step into the spotlight or take bold, public action. It wasn't even my sibling who had been lost, but a cousin. Yet, there I was, doing everything in my power to challenge the justice system.

One day, while working on the website with a friend, she looked at me and said, "I don't know what's gotten into you. Last week, you were just sad about the situation, but now you're taking action. What changed?" I told her about the Life Activation. We both paused, looked at each other, and realized: This is what it did.

The results were extraordinary. Through my efforts, the original plea deal was thrown out—an almost impossible outcome in cases like this. Although the final sentencing didn't deliver the justice my family had hoped for, the impact of our work was undeniable. We shed light on a flawed system, brought attention to my cousin's story, and, most importantly, I stepped out of my comfort zone in a way that felt profoundly important on a soul level.

Reflecting on that time, I realize the Life Activation opened doors within me that I hadn't even known were closed. It gave me the courage to act, problem-solve, and believe that I could make a difference. Even when the outcome wasn't what

I'd hoped for, I knew I had done everything I could. Without the Activation, I might have carried the heavy regret of never trying. Since then, this newfound courage has shown up in other areas of my life. I made another bold move: I sold my house and purchased a new space for my business. Owning the space instead of renting was a huge leap of faith, but it allowed me to create something entirely my own without compromise. It was a risk, but it was also empowering—an opportunity to shape my vision and stand in my own power.

The Life Activation didn't just spark change; it opened me to possibilities I hadn't considered before. It helped me step into a version of myself willing to take risks, embrace responsibility, and believe in my ability to create impact. For that, I am profoundly grateful.

Awakening the Soul: Kristina's Journey Through the Full Spirit Activation

Leading up to my first Full Spirit Activation, I recall feeling a mix of excitement and curiosity. I had heard that it could open my senses and allow me to experience more energy, and the idea of developing my senses felt thrilling.

At the same time, I didn't know what to expect, so I went into the session with an open mind, ready to embrace whatever came through.

The session itself was a fascinating experience. I remember being struck by the practitioner's voice—it was beautiful, grounding, and calming, yet carried an incredibly strong energy. The atmosphere felt peaceful but charged with something deeper, something transformative.

As I sat there, I could feel the presence of something significant shifting within me. It's hard to describe, but it was as if my inner self was being gently realigned. By the end of the session, I felt noticeably more grounded and calm, a state that lingered long after I had left.

Within a few hours, I noticed subtle yet profound changes in myself. My mind felt clearer, and I was able to focus in a way I hadn't been able to before.

As someone with ADHD, focus has always been a challenge for me. Sitting down to read a book or concentrate on a task often felt overwhelming, but now it was different. I found myself opening a book and feeling grounded, calm, and fully present. Words seemed to jump off the page with clarity as if I could see beyond the surface and into the deeper meanings behind them.

Over the next few days, I noticed another significant change: I could see more energy, especially in the periphery of my vision. It felt as if a new layer of awareness had been unlocked.

Colors seemed more vibrant, and there was a subtle shimmer to the world around me. It was as though I was beginning to perceive the unseen energies that flow through everything, and this heightened awareness brought a sense of wonder and connection to my surroundings.

A couple of weeks after the activation, I started to feel a strong sensation in my chest. It wasn't discomfort but rather a powerful awareness—a sense that my soul was waking up or reconnecting in a way I hadn't experienced before.

This newfound connection brought specific insights into my life, particularly regarding my relationship with my father. I began to feel an undeniable pull to address some unresolved issues and to do deeper healing work around our relationship.

Listening to this inner guidance, I sought coaching and healing to explore and mend the dynamics between us. As I worked through layers of emotions and memories, I found myself coming into a much deeper sense of acceptance and love toward him. It was a transformative process, one that brought both challenges and rewards.

Looking back, I am profoundly grateful that I listened to that inner calling, as it wasn't long after this healing journey that my father passed away. The work I did to heal and strengthen our bond while he was alive has been a tremendous source of peace and comfort as I navigate the journey of grief. Knowing that I could reconcile and honor our relationship has made all the difference in my healing process.

Beyond the emotional shifts, the Full Spirit Activation also brought about physical awareness and healing. I began noticing tension and pain in my jaw that I hadn't fully acknowledged. It became clear that this pain was tied to unprocessed anger, an emotion I had suppressed for a long time.

As I leaned into this awareness and took ownership of what I needed to address, the jaw pain began to dissipate significantly. It was a powerful reminder of how deeply our emotions are intertwined with our physical bodies and how releasing emotional blocks can bring relief and balance to our systems.

Another remarkable shift I noticed was in my nervous system. It felt more balanced, as if a sense of calm and equilibrium had taken root within me. Before the activation, I often felt on edge, as if my body was stuck in a constant state of fight-or-flight.

Now, there was a noticeable ease, a sense of being more in tune with myself and the world around me. This newfound balance allowed me to approach life with greater clarity and resilience.

When I received my second Full Spirit Activation a couple of years later, the experience deepened even further. The day after the session, I sat down to meditate and had the most vivid, clear meditation of my life. It was as if an intricate piece of artwork appeared, so detailed and lifelike that I could zoom in and examine every tiny element.

The level of clarity was astounding, and it felt like a window into a new dimension of spiritual perception had been opened. This meditation wasn't just a one-time experience; it was a sign that my spiritual senses had been expanded and that this heightened awareness would continue to be available to me.

Reflecting on both activations, I see how each builds upon the other, opening up new layers of growth and understanding. The first activation brought grounding, clarity, and emotional healing, while the second deepened my spiritual connection and enhanced my ability to perceive and engage with the unseen world. Together, they have been instrumental in helping me align with my true self and navigate life with greater authenticity and purpose.

One of the most profound aspects of the Full Spirit Activation has been how it has aligned my intentions and behaviors. Before the activation, I often found myself stuck in patterns where I would set an intention but struggle to follow through with the necessary actions. This disconnect created frustration and a sense of being out of sync with my goals.

After the activation, however, I noticed a shift. My intentions felt more grounded, and the actions needed to support them came with greater ease and clarity. It was as if the barriers holding me back were dissolving, allowing me to move forward with confidence and purpose.

The journey of the Full Spirit Activation is one of continuous blossoming. Each session opens new doors and reveals new layers of growth and possibility. It's not a one-time event but an ongoing process of transformation and awakening.

Through this journey, I've come to understand myself more deeply, heal old wounds, and step into a more authentic and empowered version of myself. The activation has been a catalyst for profound change in my life, and I am endlessly grateful for the gifts it has brought.

Awakening to My Inner Power–Stephan's Journey Through Life Activation and Full Spirit Activation

Before my Life Activation, I had no specific expectations. My hope was to experience life differently—whether that meant gaining a new perspective, solving problems more effectively, or even experiencing physical healing that I hadn't anticipated.

I knew the possibilities were vast, but I consciously let go of expectations. Although I desired certain changes in my life, I understood that reconnecting with my divine blueprint might shift those priorities or even render them irrelevant.

During the Life Activation, I felt a profound connection with my nervous system. It was as though energy was actively moving through my body—a sensation I've experienced during Network Spinal work, but this was more pronounced.

Over the first few days, I felt an uplifting, positive energy. Physically, I felt great. However, as the days went on, unresolved emotions and memories I thought I had dealt with began to surface. It was as if everything had been shaken up, and this process frustrated me at first. I had done so much hard work to address these old aspects of myself, and yet here they were again. Despite this, I remained calm, trusting there was something valuable to learn in revisiting these experiences.

Looking back, I realize the Life Activation brought a profound shift. Life feels easier now. I've developed a calm confidence, allowing me to embrace each day without forcing outcomes.

Previously, I would set numerous goals for my business, relationships, and personal life, only to feel overwhelmed and to question my ability to achieve them.

Now, when challenges arise, I quickly return to a state of peace and perspective, whereas before, it might have taken weeks, months, or even years. This newfound ease has transformed how I approach life. I'm more present, more joyful, and more at peace. I feel unchained and free, living on a higher internal level.

After experiencing the Life Activation, I became curious about the Full Spirit Activation. While these healings were unlike anything I had encountered, I trusted Wendy and her guidance. That trust helped me overcome any resistance I felt and take the next step. I had already accepted the reality of Reiki, so I thought, "Why not explore this as well?" The decision to proceed proved to be transformative.

One of the most significant changes has been with my singing and my relationship with my voice. Many singers explore their voices and reach milestones, but for me, the change was deeply personal. I used to feel uncertain and lacked the energy to practice consistently.

Now, I feel a calm confidence and a desire to practice regularly. I've developed discipline, consistency, and playfulness in my approach, which extends beyond singing into all aspects of my life. Where I once leaned toward cynicism with occasional bursts of optimism, I now feel curious and joyful.

Another profound shift has been in my perspective on helping others. Before, I felt an overwhelming need to heal the entire world. I would envision performing Reiki on everyone or even the entire universe.

But after these healings, my focus turned inward. I realized that by working on myself and becoming the best version of me, I could positively influence those around me without trying to control or fix them. I noticed people standing taller and becoming healthier simply by being in my presence. This was a reflection of my inner power radiating outward.

Finally, I recently faced a situation that highlighted how much I've grown. In the past, I would have passively endured someone's verbal berating, lowering my head and internalizing the hurt.

But this time, I stood in my power. I confronted the individual, and while they continued their insults, I left the situation feeling empowered. This experience showed me that I now have the strength to confront people and situations that don't align with my joy and sense of safety. It was a moment of true transformation and affirmed the incredible impact these healings have had on my life.

Empower Thyself: A Journey of Transformation for Teresa

The day of the Empower Thyself class felt like a battle before I even left the house. I was having issues with my family, and it was a huge hurdle just to leave. Then, as I was driving, a wave of nausea hit me so strongly that I considered pulling over. I sipped some water, breathed deeply, and managed to push through.

When I arrived at the location, the unease intensified. Walking up to the building, I felt dizzy, the urge to turn back tugging at me. But I'd already paid for the class, so I resolved to stick it out.

I had no idea what to expect, no idea why I was even feeling this way—it was just a class, after all, right? Yet everything about getting there felt like a test of my resolve.

Once inside, I began to settle into the experience. The material was intriguing, building upon things I'd learned before, yet also challenging my old perceptions.

Some concepts felt familiar as if I'd always known them but had forgotten. Others stretched me, asking me to reconsider deeply ingrained beliefs. One key idea we discussed resonated profoundly, yet I couldn't fully process it in the moment—it was as if the understanding needed to marinate in my mind.

The next morning, I nearly didn't go back. I still felt uneasy and unsure if this was the right path for me. But I went anyway, determined to see it through. Day two was where things began to click. As the teachings unfolded, more began to feel familiar.

By the time we reached the initiation, the dizziness and nausea returned, almost overwhelming me. I pushed through once more, trusting that there was something important happening, even if I couldn't articulate it yet.

A few weeks later, clarity hit me like a light switch. I was at another family gathering, chatting with people, when I suddenly saw the dynamics of relationships in a new way.

It was as if the curtains had been pulled back, revealing the raw truth of how I'd been interacting with others—and my part in those dynamics. I could see what needed to change and who I wanted to be moving forward.

It was both exhilarating and humbling. I realized I'd spent years allowing others to shape who I was, often at the expense of my authenticity. Now, I was seeing the threads of my relationships with new eyes—what was serving me, what wasn't, and how I could show up as a better version of myself. It was a profound shift.

From then on, I became more intentional in my interactions. I listened more, spoke less, and chose my words with care. At social events, I found myself observing people, discerning whether their energy resonated with mine before engaging. My husband asked me why I wasn't talking much at a recent party. I told him I was listening and evaluating who I wanted to connect with.

The ripple effects were undeniable. My husband, without any prompting, began taking steps to improve his health. I felt a deep sense of protection and purpose, knowing the rituals I'd learned were supporting me.

Empower Thyself didn't just teach me concepts—it gave me tools to live intentionally, to discern what serves my highest good, and to engage with the world on a deeper level. It reshaped how I interact with others, how I make decisions, and, most importantly, how I see myself.

FOUNDATIONAL TEACHINGS OF THE MODERN MYSTERY SCHOOL

Lineage of King Salomon

The Modern Mystery School (MMS) traces its teachings to the wisdom preserved by King Salomon over 3,000 years ago. Salomon gathered master healers, mystics, and spiritual leaders from around the world to unify and refine knowledge into a system for human empowerment. This lineage emphasizes the direct, unbroken transmission of teachings from teacher to student.

Significance: The lineage ensures the integrity of the teachings, maintaining their potency and alignment with universal truths.

Empowerment Through Initiation

Initiation is central to the MMS path. Through the Empower Thyself program and subsequent levels of initiation, individuals are energetically aligned with the Will of God, Nature, and the Universe. This alignment accelerates spiritual growth and offers protection and increased capacity to hold light.

Difference: While other spiritual paths may offer initiatory rites, MMS initiation connects the individual to a lineage with direct ties to ancient traditions, providing access to a broader energetic framework.

The Universal Hermetic Ray Kabbalah

The MMS teaches an experiential form of Kabbalah, emphasizing practical application for self-discovery and transformation. Participants ascend the Tree of Life, uncovering hidden aspects of themselves while integrating spiritual truths.

Difference: Unlike purely theoretical or academic approaches, MMS Universal Hermetic Ray Kabbalah combines ancient wisdom with actionable practices tailored to modern life.

Sacred Geometry and Energy Work

MMS teachings include the magick of sacred geometry, emphasizing how universal patterns govern creation and how they can be applied for healing and transformation. Students also learn energy techniques, such as the Life Activation, which awakens dormant DNA and expands spiritual potential.

Difference: Many spiritual paths focus on mindfulness or abstract metaphysical concepts, while MMS emphasizes hands-on energy work and practical tools for spiritual advancement.

Light and Darkness: The Duality of Existence

The MMS teaches that light and darkness are powerful, real forces that exist both within us and in the world around us. Darkness, often misunderstood or overlooked in other teachings, is something that must be confronted and dealt with.

The MMS path guides individuals to face these aspects within themselves to eliminate the darkness and expand the light within, leading to greater spiritual growth and self-mastery.

Difference: Unlike some New Age philosophies, which dismiss the concept of darkness or emphasize only positivity, the MMS emphasizes the critical role of discernment—the ability to recognize and address the forces that shape our inner and outer realities. It also stresses personal accountability in confronting darkness, ensuring we take responsibility for transforming it rather than avoiding it.

Magick and Rituals

The MMS offers a wide range of teachings, including Enochian magick, Egyptian magick, Viking Magick, and more, in addition to ceremonial rituals. These practices aim to create a direct connection with divine forces and foster spiritual growth.

Difference: Many paths treat magick as symbolic or metaphorical, while MMS magick is approached as a science and art meant to be actively practiced and experienced.

Know Thyself

Self-mastery and self-discovery are at the core of the MMS path. By uncovering one's true essence, individuals learn to live in alignment with their divine purpose.

Difference: While many spiritual traditions encourage self-reflection, the MMS provides structured tools, teachings, and rituals to facilitate profound personal transformation.

How the Modern Mystery School Differs from Other Spiritual Paths

Focus on Empowerment and Personal Responsibility

The MMS emphasizes that individuals are the creators of their reality. While healers and teachers provide support, the individual must actively engage with their healing and growth.

Difference: Other paths may focus on surrender or reliance on external forces for enlightenment, while MMS fosters active participation in one's spiritual journey.

Unbroken Lineage and Sacred Authority

Unlike many modern spiritual paths that draw inspiration from multiple sources, the MMS teachings stem from a direct, unbroken lineage, ensuring purity and consistency.

Difference: This contrasts with eclectic or non-lineage-based traditions, which may lack the depth and energetic connection of a unified system.

A Structured Path of Progression

The MMS provides a step-by-step framework for spiritual advancement, from Empower Thyself to advanced levels of initiation, such as Healer, Ritual Master, and Ipsissimus. Each step builds on the previous, creating a clear and cohesive journey or path of progression.

Difference: Many spiritual paths lack this level of structure, leaving practitioners to navigate their growth without a defined roadmap.

Direct Experience over Dogma

The MMS encourages direct interaction with spiritual truths through rituals, meditations, initiations, healings, and energy work rather than adhering to rigid doctrines or belief systems.

Difference: Some traditions rely heavily on scripture or philosophy, whereas MMS emphasizes experiential learning and self-discovery.

Integration of Ancient and Modern Wisdom

While rooted in ancient traditions, the MMS adapts its teachings to modern-day challenges, offering practical tools for navigating contemporary life.

Difference: Other paths may either cling to tradition or focus entirely on modern approaches, lacking the synthesis that MMS offers.

Community and Support

The MMS fosters a global community of practitioners, providing mentorship, training, and support for those on the path.

Difference: While many spiritual paths are solitary or lack organized infrastructure, MMS provides a robust network to guide and sustain students.

The Modern Mystery School path offers a profound opportunity for individuals to connect with their divine purpose, overcome limitations, and contribute to the healing and evolution of humanity. By aligning with a lineage dedicated to the service of light, students experience accelerated growth, deeper clarity, and a sense of purpose that transcends the individual.

This path is not just about personal enlightenment—it's about becoming a beacon of light for others, helping to create a ripple effect that uplifts the collective consciousness. Through initiation, teachings, and direct experience, the MMS empowers individuals to step fully into their roles as co-creators of a brighter, more harmonious world.

The History of MMS

The Modern Mystery School started in 1997 when Founder Gudni Gudnason brought the Lineage of King Salomon out of the realm of the secret and was allowed to open the school to the public.

It has steadily grown over the last 29 years. As of 2025, there have been 43,757 initiates, 478 healers, 324 teachers, and practitioners in 55 different countries. Currently, the North American headquarters is in Toronto, Canada, and the Eastern World headquarters is in Japan.

Certified practitioners and teachers can be found all over the world. The school's website has a searchable section so that you can find a practitioner in your community. The website is: modernmysteryschoolint.com/certified-professionals/.

Higher-level classes, second-step initiations, and Ritual Master classes are taught at the worldwide headquarters, and some are taught by international teachers at other locations. Many classes such as the first step initiation called Empower Thyself are taught by Guides at their home healing centers.

A documentary shares stories of students who have taken the Empower Thyself class and walked the path of healings, teachings, and training with the Modern Mystery School. The link can be found on the Modern Mystery School International's website or YouTube page.

My Relationship to the Modern Mystery School

I have taken numerous classes and earned certifications to offer a variety of healings and teachings through the Modern Mystery School. These profound teachings have not only transformed my life but also allowed me to share this powerful work with others. At my healing center, I provide many of these services to those who feel called to explore their healing and growth.

The scope of the Modern Mystery School's teachings is immense, far beyond what any single practitioner can offer. While I provide a range of transformative healings, the school offers many additional modalities and advanced teachings. If clients feel inspired to continue their journey, they can travel to Modern Mystery School centers located around the world, including Canada, England, Brazil, South Africa, and Japan. It's always an option, never a requirement.

Some classes have prerequisites, such as foundational courses, that lay the groundwork for deeper teachings, but these are designed to ensure a progressive and aligned path.

I am also committed to my growth and continue to advance by attending new training and classes every year. Additionally, as part of the Modern Mystery School's professional standards, I am required to recertify annually in key foundational healings and teachings, such as the **Life Activation, Full Spirit Activation,** and the **Empower Thyself** class. This ensures I can channel the energy for these healings and classes with precision and integrity.

Beyond these foundational offerings, I have a diverse tool-box of healing modalities that I share with my clients. These include:

- Etheric Reconstruction
- Sacred Geometry Healings
- Baby Blessing
- Soul Retrieval
- Hermetic Re-Balancing
- Ensofic Ray Reiki
- King Salomon Healing modalities
- Spiritual Drug Detox
- Ra Protection Healing
- Holy God Matrix Realignment
- Archangel Compassion Summoning
- Hands of Melchizedek Healing
- Hexagram Healing
- Laying of Hands
- Spirit Infusion
- Celestial Code
- Starseed Healing

... and much more. Each healing is designed to address specific aspects of an individual's journey, helping them uncover their true potential and align with their highest purpose.

Through the Modern Mystery School, I am honored to be a guide, healer, and teacher, supporting others as they embark on their transformative journeys.

Behind the Titles

It's important to clarify the structure of the Modern Mystery School for those who are curious. Mystery Schools have existed for thousands of years, often hidden from society because humanity, for much of that time, wasn't ready to embrace the truth of who they are.

The Modern Mystery School traces its lineage back over 3,000 years to the teachings of King Salomon, with knowledge passed from teacher to student through the sacred process of initiation.

This direct transmission of wisdom has preserved the integrity and honor of the Mystery School tradition, which holds ancient secrets about the universe, our divine nature, and the keys to true spiritual empowerment.

Today, this knowledge is available to all who seek it and are willing to honor it. Every lineage has individuals who anchor and uphold it on the planet, with the authority to offer teachings to those who seek the light.

In the Modern Mystery School, these individuals are part of the Third Order. They are titled "Sovereign" because each one holds all the keys of the lineage and could lead the school independently if needed.

The title "Ipsissimus" represents one of the highest ranks of initiation within MMS. An Ipsissimus has mastered not only their own life but also the universal laws of creation. They embody pure will, consciousness, and divine alignment, often serving as a teacher or guide to others on their spiritual journey. Ipsissima is the feminine form of the title.

When you hear these titles, you can think of them as indicators of spiritual attainment, much like the way the military ranks of admiral or lieutenant indicate levels of authority and experience. They no longer need a teacher.

The Third Order is comprised of Founder Gudni Gudnason, Sovereign Ipsissimus Hideto Nakagome, and Sovereign Ipsissimus Dave Lanyon.

Founder Gudni Gudnason, a Sovereign Ipsissimus, is honored with the title "Founder" for creating the Modern Mystery School after publicly sharing the teachings from the secret inner Mystery School lineage of King Salomon in 1997.

He was initiated into the Mysteries in the Great Pyramid of Giza and is an initiated Celtic Medicine Man, Viking Shaman, Druid Priest, Templar Knight, and Egyptian High Priest of Isis.

Gudni has traveled worldwide, teaching individuals to awaken to the possibility of World Peace and to discover joy in life while coming to know themselves. He built the Modern Mystery School from the ground up after moving to Utah in 1997. With the help of Sovereign Ipsissimus Dave Lanyon and Sovereign Ipsissimus Hideto Nakagome, it has expanded to 55 countries.

Gudni currently resides in Japan with his wife, Ipsissima Divina Eiko Gudnason, supporting the global growth of the Mystery School, transitioning from administration to the role of Hierophant, a Master Teacher for students at the highest levels.

If you have the opportunity to take a class with him, you'll experience his remarkable gift for helping you discern the deeper meanings behind his captivating stories. These stories stay with you long after the class and encourage you to reflect on your understanding and beliefs about the world. You always leave the class with more clarity and questions—truly a gift to humanity and our shared desire to know ourselves.

Sovereign Ipsissimus Dave Lanyon, mentioned earlier in this book, is the leader of the Modern Mystery School North America. He runs the school from its headquarters in Toronto, Canada, where he resides with his wife, Ipsissima Divina Franca Lanyon.

With a background in business and martial arts—where he was both an instructor and a dojo owner—Sovereign Ipsissimus Dave has long been committed to teaching, coaching, and motivating others.

Once he embarked on the path of initiation, he leveraged his extensive knowledge and experience to expand the school rapidly, now reaching over 55 countries worldwide. He also leads the global Order of the Warriors of Light and holds the rank of High Priest of Egyptian Magick. As a Master of Enochian (Angel) Magick and a specialist in Viking, Celtic, and

Egyptian Shamanism, his expertise spans numerous esoteric traditions.

I've mentioned this before, but it bears repeating: I have never encountered leadership like I have with Sovereign Ipsissimus Dave Lanyon. He is unapologetically himself and firmly holds the line, yet he remains approachable and deeply supportive of his team.

He doesn't seek power for its own sake but commands it naturally. His authenticity as a leader is something I've never experienced before and that is a reflection of the power of the lineage and the teachings of the school.

Sovereign Ipsissimus Hideto Nakagome recognized the importance of the Modern Mystery School's mission for World Peace and has been eager to support this endeavor. Coming from a pure Japanese Bushi (Samurai) family, he channels that power in his work. He is initiated as a Priest of Mikkyo Esoteric Buddhism, Viking Shaman, Celtic Shaman, Knight Templar, Egyptian Shaman, and more.

Sovereign Ipsissimus Hideto has authored several successful metaphysical books in Japan and serves as the head instructor of the Ensofic Ray Institute. He lives in Japan with his wife, Ipsissima Divina Luisa Nakagome. He teaches with fun and humor, sharing his wealth of wisdom in all his classes.

There is a video of the three of them speaking about the school on YouTube: youtube.com/watch?v=op7aLi8Ueek&t=1408s

In 2022, there were seven new Ipsissimus initiated into the school, and in 2024, there were four more Ipsissimus initiated:

Governing Ipsissimus

Ipsissima Divina Franca Lanyon—Ipsissimus of Alchemy

Ipsissima Divina Theresa Bullard-Whyke—Ipsissimus of Kabbalah

Ipsissima Divina Luisa Nakagome—Ipsissimus of Shamanism

Ipsissima Divina Eiko Gudnason—Ipsissimus of the Royal Way

Ipsissima Divina Tsukiko Kimura—Ipsissimus of the Ensofic Ray

Ipsissima Azusa Yoda—Grand Oracle

Honorary Ipsissima Sandra Reed

Honorary Ipsissima Verla Wade

Ipsissima Kathleen Lanyon—Ipsissima of the Governance of the Light

Ipsissima Liza Rossi—Ipsissima of the Divine Arts

Ipsissima Kate Bartram-Brown—Ipsissima of the Noble Arts

Leadership Council

There is also a council of 12 women—six from the Western world and six from the Eastern world. They provide leadership for the lineage and work with the Third Order and the Hierarchy of Light. Currently serving on the Council of 12:

WEST

Ipsissima Divina Franca Lanyon

Ipsissima Divina Theresa Bullard

Ipsissima Divina Liza Rossi

Ipsissima Divina Kate Bartram-Brown

Divina Rita van den Berg

Divina Ann Donnelly

EAST

Ipsissima Divina Eiko Gudnason

Ipsissima Divina Luisa Nakagome

Ipsissima Divina Tsukiko Kimura

Ipsissima Divina Yoda Asuza

Divina Maki Otani

Divina Suzuki Kitamura

A title Divina is an honorific bestowed upon female leaders who have attained a high level of spiritual mastery and responsibility within the organization. They serve as international instructors, guides, and healers, dedicating their lives to empowering individuals through ancient wisdom and modern spiritual practices. Their roles often encompass teaching advanced classes, leading healing sessions, and mentoring students on their spiritual journeys.

I am often asked why no women are leading the school. From an outside perspective, it may seem like the leadership consists of three men at the top, with a council of women below them.

Given many people's experiences in the workplace or in life, this can look like the familiar hierarchical structure designed to disempower women—a kind of glass ceiling.

However, in reality, the Third Order works closely with the Governing Ipsissimus and the leadership council on most matters. For any structure to function effectively, both masculine and feminine energies must be in balance. The masculine represents action and force, while the feminine is the womb of creation. The feminine creates, and the masculine brings that creation into the world.

This balance is central to the school's structure. The women in leadership hold very high-level responsibilities, and I don't believe they feel constrained by a glass ceiling. They understand that their talents are valued, and if they seek more responsibility, it is offered if it is appropriate to their path.

Response to Criticism

If you have ever searched for the Modern Mystery School online, you might have come across articles or stories portraying it in a negative light. One particular article accused the leadership of being cult-like figures with hidden agendas, manipulating students for selfish reasons.

When this article came out, I had already attended Healers Academy and was in the middle of my Kabbalah ascension. I had never met Founder Gudni or Sovereign Ipsissimus Hideto, and although I had only briefly encountered Sovereign Ipsissimus Dave during Healers Academy, I had no personal experience to support the claims being made.

What stood out was that the article did not mention anything about the healings or the classes—the very heart of the school's work. Instead, it focused solely on attacking the leadership, which I found curious.

Later in a class, it was explained that the publication behind the article had approached the school for comment. The leadership agreed to an interview, but only if the conversation could be recorded and they could review the article before publication to ensure their words were accurately represented. The publication refused. That struck me as odd and raised more questions about the intentions behind the piece.

Having spent more time in the Modern Mystery School since then, I've never seen the leadership act in the way the article described. My personal experience has been one of empowerment and transformation, both spiritually and emotionally.

I believe that, unfortunately, people are often programmed to distrust or criticize what they don't understand, especially if it challenges their established beliefs or societal norms. This type of resistance is common when something represents light and positivity, as it can force people to confront uncomfortable truths about themselves or the world.

I've even heard a rumor that the author of that article had a personal motive—supposedly, he had been dating someone who attended the school, and after taking a few classes, she broke up with him. It was suggested that she felt empowered by what she learned and decided to end the relationship, which might have inspired him to write the article out of anger. I can't confirm whether that's true, but it makes sense when you consider how personal biases can shape public opinions.

I've come to realize that things aligned with the light often challenge the status quo, forcing individuals to transform, heal, or reflect on their current state. Not everyone is ready to embrace that change—it can be uncomfortable or even threatening to their identity.

Light shines on the areas where growth is needed, but some people aren't prepared to face those aspects of themselves. In a world where personal gain often drives people's actions, it's difficult for many to believe that something could genuinely be for the collective good.

This skepticism is amplified when people encounter something that feels too selfless or altruistic because it contradicts the narratives they've been taught about the world.

Additionally, encountering something positive and aligned with the light can trigger unresolved issues or shadow aspects within individuals. They may project their internal fears, doubts, or insecurities onto the very thing that is positive, simply because it stirs something uncomfortable within them.

Despite the criticism, the light continues to create profound transformations in those open to it. Often, the skepticism comes from people's internal limitations and wounds. But those who can see beyond those barriers recognize and appreciate the genuine benefits offered by the Modern Mystery School.

It's also important to note that participation in the classes and healings is always voluntary. There are certain requirements to stay certified, but these are choices, never obligations. For me, the journey through the Modern Mystery School has been one of profound personal empowerment and healing, regardless of what detractors may say.

EPILOGUE

I emphasized earlier in this book and throughout our discussion of this path that everyone's results will be unique. My results will not mirror yours because we are distinct, cosmic beings, shaped by our purpose, experiences, and path.

The light we encounter on this journey will touch us differently depending on what we are ready and willing to heal. And that's not only okay—it's how it's meant to be.

For some, the timing isn't right to embrace healing or the light that flows in. They may turn away from it, consciously or unconsciously, until they are ready. There is no judgment; healing is deeply personal, and readiness is a sacred, individual choice.

One of the most profound teachings we learn as healers is that all healing is self-healing. At the heart of every transformation is the individual. My role as a healer is to facilitate the process—to prepare the energy, hold space with intention and compassion, and provide support through tools and rituals. But the power of true transformation resides within the individual's innate ability to heal, whether physically, mentally, emotionally, or spiritually.

Healing is not a passive process; it is an active engagement. It requires a person to take responsibility for their well-being by making conscious choices that support their healing journey. These choices include cultivating healthier habits, using the tools or rituals provided, addressing emotional wounds, or finding balance in their daily lives.

Consider the example of a physical wound. When you get a cut, your body initiates its natural healing mechanisms: clotting, tissue repair, and regeneration. External aids like bandages or antiseptics can assist in this process, but ultimately, your body does the work of healing.

This same principle applies to emotional and spiritual healing. As a healer, I may create a sacred space and facilitate the energy required for transformation, but the individual must choose to delve within and complete the inner work. They must confront old wounds, release attachments, or embrace change.

Acknowledging that not everyone is ready to take these steps is important. Some individuals may find it more comfortable to remain where they are, within the familiarity of their current circumstances. That's perfectly okay, too. There is always a choice, and there is always another opportunity to heal when they are ready.

A healer is not a fixer. I do not "fix" people or "make" their transformation happen. Instead, I am a facilitator, guide, and supportive presence. I provide tools, energetic support, and insight to help create an environment where healing can occur. But the ultimate outcome depends on the individual's openness, willingness, and readiness to heal.

This is the essence of **Innerpowerment**: placing the individual at the center of their healing journey. It's about recognizing that healing is not passively received from an external source. It is an active, participatory process—a co-creation between the individual, the energy of the Universe, and the divine light within them.

When we take responsibility for our healing, we reclaim our power. We step into a space of self-awareness and self-mastery, where the potential for growth, transformation, and empowerment becomes limitless.

This path is not always easy, but it is profoundly rewarding. For those who are ready, the journey of healing and self-discovery can illuminate the deepest truths of who we are and what we can become.

RESOURCES FOR YOUR JOURNEY

Inspired to take the next step? Let's connect!

If my journey has sparked something within you—a flicker of inspiration, a desire to ignite your inner flame—I'd be honored to connect with you.

I'd love to learn more about who you are, your unique path, and what you're seeking. I'm here to guide and support you on your journey of spiritual growth and healing, sharing insights that have transformed my life.

Everything I've achieved and discovered is within reach for you, too, if you choose this path. The journey to *Know Thyself* is open to all, a path meant to reignite your eternal flame and bring you to a place of joy, passion, empowerment, self-mastery, and inner peace.

Are you inspired to take the next step? Schedule a Life Activation.

If you are ready to unlock your true potential and step into a life of greater purpose, joy, and fulfillment, I invite you to schedule a Life Activation. This powerful process will align your energy with your highest potential, clearing blockages and awakening your divine essence.

It is the first step to:

- Activate your inner power.
- Gain clarity on your path.
- Begin the transformative journey toward self-mastery.

Schedule this in-person session now: wendybenningswanson. com/schedule-a-life-activation

Or use this QR code:

If you would like to talk more about this path, schedule Your *FREE Personalized Consultation.*

Every individual's path is unique, and I'd love to help you uncover yours. I'm offering a free hour-long consultation where we can:

- Explore where you are on your spiritual journey.
- Identify blocks that may be holding you back.
- Discuss personalized next steps to help you align with your true purpose.

Whether you're ready for healing, initiation, or simply want to learn more about how this path can help you, this consultation is an opportunity to connect and start moving forward.

Schedule your consultation here: wendybenningswanson.com/ free-consultation

Or Use this QR Code:

If you are still curious but not ready to start, download this free resource: Empowerment Toolkit.

Unlock your Empowerment Toolkit, a collection of tools and practices designed to help you:

- Reduce stress and declutter your mind.
- Begin incorporating daily rituals for spiritual growth.
- Gain clarity and confidence in your next steps.

This downloadable guide includes practical exercises, journaling prompts, and simple meditations to support you on your journey.

Download your Empowerment Toolkit now: wendybenning-swanson.com/empowerment-toolkit

Use this QR code:

If you would like to find a Life Activation Practitioner in your local area, visit the Modern Mystery School website and look under the section titled: Certified Professionals: modernmysteryschoolint.com/certified-professionals

YOUR CALL TO ACTION: STEP INTO EMPOWERMENT

The power to create profound change in your life is already within you. This path involves uncovering that power, embracing your unique light, and stepping into your authentic self.

If you are ready to take the next step, visit my website for a list of healing modalities and upcoming events. You can schedule a Life Activation to begin your journey.

Together, we can illuminate the way forward and help you create a life filled with purpose, joy, and empowerment.

Take your next step today at wendybenningswanson.com.

ACKNOWLEDGMENTS

I would like to acknowledge my first Guide, Sarah Smriga (Gebeke). Thank you for choosing the light and giving me the opportunity to do the same.

Sovereign Ipsissimus Dave Lanyon and Ipsissima Divina Franca Lanyon, thank you for all you do to hold the light and create a space for us to learn and grow.

In addition, with deep gratitude and reverence, I acknowledge Sovereign Ipsissimus Dave Lanyon for his unwavering dedication to truth, empowerment, and self-mastery. Through his teachings in the Modern Mystery School, he has illuminated a path that has forever changed my life. His ability to balance wisdom, strength, and compassion has shown me what true leadership looks like—one that challenges, inspires, and calls forth the highest potential in those willing to walk the path.

It is through his guidance that I have gained a deeper understanding of discernment, Will, and the courage required to confront both light and darkness within. His presence in this world is a testament to what it means to stand in service to humanity with integrity and purpose.

For his teachings, his example, and the profound impact he has had on my journey, I am eternally grateful.

With deep gratitude and admiration, I acknowledge Ipsissima Divina Franca Lanyon for her unwavering dedication, grace, and embodiment of divine feminine strength. Her presence is a force of wisdom, compassion, and power—one that inspires those walking the path of self-mastery to rise to their highest potential.

Her teachings and leadership have shown me the depth of true empowerment—not through force, but through the mastery of self, the refinement of Will, and the courage to embrace both light and darkness with unwavering clarity. Beyond her wisdom, I also deeply appreciate her warmth and ability to uplift others with kindness and strength.

For her guidance, her example, and the profound impact she has had on my journey, I am truly grateful.

With profound gratitude, I acknowledge Founder Gudni Gudnason for his vision, dedication, and unwavering commitment to the mission of world service. Through his creation of the Modern Mystery School, he has preserved and shared the sacred teachings that have transformed my life and the lives of countless others. His courage to walk this path, despite all obstacles, is an inspiration to those seeking truth, empowerment, and enlightenment.

Because of his work, I have been given the opportunity to truly *Know Myself*—to awaken my divine essence, claim my Will, and walk with greater clarity and purpose. His teachings have ignited a deep remembrance of who I am and the power that resides within each of us to create real and lasting change in this world.

For his wisdom, his sacrifices, and his enduring legacy, I offer my deepest gratitude.

With deep respect and gratitude, I acknowledge Sovereign Ipsissimus Hideto Nakagome for his unwavering dedication to the sacred path of empowerment and enlightenment. His mastery, discipline, and devotion to the Great Work are an inspiration to all who seek true self-mastery. Through his presence and teachings, I have witnessed the power of precision, integrity, and the relentless pursuit of excellence in service to humanity.

Beyond his immense wisdom and leadership, I also deeply appreciate his humor. His ability to weave sharp wit into profound lessons makes the path all the more engaging, reminding us that even in the most intense moments of growth, laughter is a powerful force. His unique blend of strength, wisdom, and lightheartedness is truly a gift.

For his wisdom, his strength, and his embodiment of the ancient teachings, I am profoundly grateful.

With deep gratitude, I want to thank Ipsissima Divina Theresa Bullard. Her presence on the Gaia TV show *Open Minds* opened a door I didn't even know I was searching for. That single conversation was the spark that lit the fire within me—a fire that led me on a path of healing, awakening, and transformation.

I am profoundly thankful for everything she endured, studied, and embodied to be in that moment, on that show, sharing her truth. It changed my life.

ABOUT THE AUTHOR

Wendy Benning Swanson lives in the Twin Cities area of Minnesota with her husband, two kids, and two rambunctious dogs.

After the passing of her first husband, Wendy faced a profound turning point in her life. Determined to create stability for her family, she founded a staffing firm and devoted nine years to building it into a successful enterprise.

Yet, despite her achievements, Wendy felt an undeniable pull that this work no longer aligned with her deeper purpose. She found herself questioning what truly mattered and seeking meaning beyond the responsibilities of her professional and personal life.

This inner unrest sparked a journey of self-reflection that led Wendy to explore life, death, and her identity within these profound realms. She delved into personal growth and healing, navigating her grief and the sense of being stuck that accompanied it. Her search for answers and transformation eventually guided her to the Modern Mystery School, where she began receiving healing sessions that deeply resonated with her soul.

Through these experiences, Wendy realized that her true path had always been self-discovery—a journey of knowing herself at the deepest level. This awakening inspired her to take the next steps in her spiritual evolution, leading to her initiation into the Modern Mystery School tradition. Over time, she became certified as a healer, teacher, and guide, acquiring the tools and knowledge to help others on their paths of transformation.

Wendy's journey wasn't without challenges. She faced her inner critic, self-doubt, and the pervasive feeling of being stuck, yet she persevered with the curiosity and courage to seek something more. Each step she took revealed new layers of healing and empowerment, allowing her to shed old patterns and align with her true essence.

Today, Wendy is wholeheartedly committed to supporting others in uncovering their divine potential. She believes that healing and transformation are accessible to everyone willing to embark on the path of self-discovery.

At her healing center, she offers a variety of services, including energy healings, spiritual teachings, and transformative classes, all designed to help individuals reconnect with their true selves and step into their purpose.

Wendy's work is deeply rooted in her belief that each person is a unique and powerful being who can heal, grow, and transform their life. Through her book, teachings, and healings, she aims to inspire others to take that first step to knowing themselves, embracing their light, and living a life filled with joy, purpose, and inner peace.